Here's What These Christian Leaders Say

"Few things are more important than helpful words of encouragement along the road. Lareau Lindquist has been doing this through his *Encouragement* letters. Now to have these in a book is wonderfully helpful. I heartily commend *Too Soon To Quit*."

Ted W. Engstrom
President Emeritus
World Vision

"No title for a letter or book could be more precise and comprehensive than *Too Soon To Quit*. This book of encouragement will be just that for its readers."

Richard C. Halverson
Chaplain
United States Senate

"I know first hand the great encouragement Lareau Lindquist has been to so many. *Too Soon To Quit* will be an encouragement to us all to keep on keeping on."

Elaine Townsend
Ambassador at Large
Wycliffe Bible Translators

"In an age of cynicism and unprecedented pressures, who doesn't need a Barnabas from time to time? Lareau Lindquist's life and worldwide ministry embody this gift of encouragement. *Too Soon To Quit* will enrich an ever-widening circle of friends."

Dr. John Gration
Professor of Missions
Wheaton College Graduate School

"Read this book and be blessed. Lareau Lindquist is God's gift of encouragement to a host of God's people around the world. He brings blessing wherever he goes. Let his words be God's words of encouragement to you."

Dr. Wesley L. Duewel
President Emeritus
OMS International, Inc.

"On every page you will receive hope, insight, reassurance, and a challenge to trust God. Reading this book over several months will lift your spirit and enable you to live your life with meaning and joy."

Jim and Sally Conway
Authors and Founders
Mid-Life Dimensions

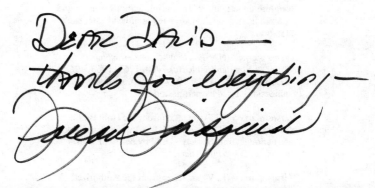

Dear David —
thanks for everything —
Lareau Lindquist

TOO SOON TO QUIT

Reflections on Encouragement

By
Lareau Lindquist

Published By

Quadrus Media

721 E. State Street　　Rockford, Illinois　61104

TOO SOON TO QUIT
By Lareau Lindquist

(c) 1994 Barnabas International
Edited by Joe Musser
Cover by Scott Johnson Design

Published by Quadrus Media
Rockford, Illinois 61104

Printed in the United States of America

Library of Congress Cataloging in Publication Data
Lindquist, Lareau
        Too Soon To Quit
ISBN 1-885481-00-4 (Hardcover)
ISBN 1-885481-01-2 (Paperback)
    1. General Encouragement 2. Devotional I. Title.

Dedicated to Erwin W. Parr

In 1967, my wife, Evie, and I moved to Des Moines, Iowa, where I became the pastor of the Indianola Heights Evangelical Free Church. Immediately we became close friends with "Ervie" and Catherine Parr. That friendship continued through the years until two years ago, when Ervie was called suddenly and unexpectedly into the presence of his Lord. I still miss Ervie, although our friendship with Catherine and their children continues.

I dedicate this book to Ervie's memory. We traveled often . . . and fished together . . . and golfed together . . . sang together . . . laughed . . . and prayed together. And we dreamed together about a ministry that eventually came into being, Barnabas International.

He was a very special friend. As I think of Ervie, many things come to mind. He was a Christian . . . Soul Winner (as described in one of the chapters in this book) . . . Visionary . . . *Encourager.*

Ervie helped us start Barnabas International . . . was a board member . . . and vice chairman of our small organization. He was also a musician . . . businessman . . . and benefactor to this worldwide ministry. But most of all, he was a friend. Yes . . . that's exactly the right word, in summary . . . *Friend.*

I further dedicate this book to Catherine, his wife . . . to their two children, Mrs. Cathy Brandt (and her husband, Tim), and Ron Parr (and his wife, Cheri). Each of these family members have embraced the ministry of Barnabas International, as did Ervie.

And we are so grateful!

Lareau Lindquist
March 18, 1994
Singapore

Acknowledgments

Many friends have contributed to the process of making this book a reality. I want to express my gratitude to all who had a part in this project.

> Joe Musser, longtime friend, who served as editor
> Scott Johnson, art designer for the book cover and jacket
> Dottie Campbell, typist and administrative assistant
> Cheryl Warner, coworker with Barnabas and proofreader
> Paul Cedar, my college buddy and preface *encourager*
> And my family, as we continue to look for meaningful
> > ways to help each other:

> > Evie, my wife
> > Our children . . .
> > > Jodi Strzalko, and her husband, Mike
> > > Reese
> > > Michelle
> > > Jeffrey, and his wife, Jan
> > > --and their children (our grandchildren)
> > > > Peter John and Sara Elizabeth

I also want to thank the many who regularly pray and give to the ministry of Barnabas International, without whose support we would not be able to continue. Further gratitude is expressed for the countless Christians we have met and served around the world.

I want to sincerely thank the special friends (who wish to remain anonymous) who provided the funds to make this book possible.

Lareau Lindquist

PREFACE

The ministry of encouragement is one of the most neglected today in our society. Most of us live in a climate of criticism, competition, and conflict. For many of us, a kind word or sincere compliment from someone else is rare.

Unfortunately, that same spirit has found its way into the lives of many Christians, their families--even their churches. Without realizing it, many believers have become like the Children of Israel who were constantly complaining and murmuring. How sad!

In contrast, Jesus has come to us with a spirit of love, compassion, and encouragement. That is the true spirit of Jesus--and it is the spirit which He desires for His children to enjoy--all of us who follow Him as Savior and Lord!

Barnabas was such a person in the early Church. Wherever he went, Barnabas carried on a special ministry of encouragement. In fact, he had the nickname *"son of encouragement."*

Without a doubt, my longtime friend, Lareau Lindquist, has been a contemporary Barnabas to me--and to many others. He has been a "brother of encouragement." Lareau is one of the most gifted Bible expositors and Christian leaders I have ever known. It would have been quite natural for him to have been acclimated to our culture by becoming totally immersed in his own ministry.

Instead, Lareau has been faithful in following the Lord into a much more unusual--and strategic--ministry of encouraging others. For over a decade, he and his wife, Evie, have given themselves to the ministry of encouragement around the world They spend their lives traveling to the most remote parts of the world to inspire and edify pastors, missionaries, and other servants of Jesus Christ.

In addition, Lareau extends his ministry of encouragement to multiplied thousands of us who receive his monthly letter, *Encouragement*. He is truly a Barnabas who has been, and continues to be, God's special *"son of encouragement"* to so many.

Now his ministry of encouragement is being extended in a new and wonderful way with the publication of this book. Included in its pages are many years' worth of monthly *Encouragement*. You will be blessed as you prayerfully read these uplifting insights for helpful daily living. Without a doubt . . . *you will be encouraged!*

And, when you have received some of that special inspiration from the pages of this book, I pray that you will not merely bask in the enjoyment of that experience. Instead, please *reach out* and share that encouragement with those around you. What blessing it will bring them . . . and what joy it will bring to you . . . and what glory it will bring to God! That's what this book is all about.

And that is the heartbeat of Barnabas International and of Lareau Lindquist. It is with joy and anticipation that I recommend this wonderful volume to you, with the prayer that all of us may be motivated to join with our brother in Christ in his great ministry of edification and encouragement.

Paul A. Cedar
President
Evangelical Free Church of America

Dr. Paul Cedar is an author, pastor, evangelist, and church leader who is also president of his denomination. He serves on the U.S. Lausanne Committee and is chairman of the International Coalition of "AD 2000 and Beyond" Movement. He is also a guest dean of the Billy Graham Schools of Evangelism, and serves on the boards of the International Lausanne Committee, Leighton Ford Ministries, Trinity Evangelical Divinity School, Trinity College, and Trinity Western University. In addition, Dr. Cedar serves on the advisory boards of a number of strategic mission and ministry organizations. He is the author of seven books, and has lectured in a number of seminaries and universities. Dr. Cedar and his wife, Jeannie, have three children.

INTRODUCTION

Many years ago, I heard the words of Dr. V. Raymond Edman, *"It is always too soon to quit!"*

I have often thought of these words in my own life. I've also quoted them in my preaching and writing.

There have been times . . . *many times* . . . when I have been tempted to give up. Quit. Do you identify with my feelings? Maybe wanting to quit is normal. We face pressures and stress . . . inner insecurities . . . relational problems . . . frustrations in the ministry or on the job . . . financial adjustments . . . the bungling of a loved one or coworker . . . the list goes on and on.

I remember someone saying, *"On the inside I have been tempted to quit at least a dozen times a week . . . but I have not quit."*

Two months ago, while ministering in Manila, I received a telephone call late one night from the head of a large pastors' group that I was to speak to the next day. This man said, "Please address our theme, *'Keep On Keeping On'."*

I did my best to organize my already prepared thoughts and message along the lines of that theme. Otis Skillings, team worship leader, picked up on that idea. He wrote and dedicated a theme song, with the same title, to them.

At the end of the day, the leader came up to me and said, "Thank you for encouraging us to *'Keep On Keeping On'."* We agreed that this theme might not be the most dignified way of stating the truth of our encouragement, but the reality of the message was there for all to hear. We were pleased to be of genuine inspiration to these hardworking Christian leaders.

And I think we all need to be nudged toward perseverance and persistence. Not just in ministry . . . or in our family relationships . . . in the workplace . . . in our churches . . . but in every situation, at all times. *It is always too soon to quit!*

A Word of Explanation . . .

Barnabas International is a ministry of encouragement, enrichment and edification. We are essentially committed to *serving servants*, that is--ministering to pastors, teachers, evangelists, missionaries, translators and the whole host of dedicated servants of Christ serving overseas.

Our growing staff is dedicated to teaching/preaching conferences, retreats and seminars outside the North American continent. We seek to creatively fulfill our charter to strengthen other servants through encouragement and inspiration.

The chapters of this book were written, initially, as letters of encouragement (in fact, we even called them *Encouragement*). Every month, a new *Encouragement* letter was sent to Christians serving Christ around the world. The list soon grew to *thousands* now receiving these letters.

Through the encouragement of many friends, these *Encouragement* letters have been rewritten, edited, and modified to fit the format of this book. We present them as separate chapters, for daily inspiration. At the end of the book, there is a word on how you can receive the monthly *Encouragement* letters on a regular basis.

It is our prayer that this book will be used of God to bless, encourage and strengthen *you* . . . in your home, life, church, workplace and ministry.

A NEW YEAR'S RESOLVE

It was January 1, 1989. My son Reese and I were on a TWA 767 en route from New York to Zurich. From there we were to go on to fourteen days of ministry in Europe with several different mission organizations. It was late at night, and I had just finished browsing the FINANCIAL TIMES, offered by the flight attendant. I was surprised to find inside the pages of this secular periodical a prayer, written by Samuel Johnson on January 1, 1770. I was then refreshed and challenged by these words, written 219 years earlier:

> "Almighty God, by whose mercy I am permitted to behold the beginning of another year, succor with Thy help, and bless with Thy favour, the creature whom Thou vouchsafest to preserve. Mitigate, if it shall seem best to Thee, the diseases of my body, and compose the disorders of my mind. Dispel my terrors; and grant that the time which Thou shalt yet allow me may not pass unprofitably away. Let not pleasure seduce me. Let me perform to Thy glory, and the good of my fellow-creatures, the work which Thou shalt yet appoint me; and grant that, as I draw nearer to my dissolution, I may, by the help of the Holy Spirit, feel my knowledge of Thee increased, my hope exalted, and my faith strengthened; that when the hour which is coming shall come, I may pass by a holy death to everlasting happiness, for the sake of Jesus Christ our Lord. Amen."

What a way to begin a year . . . to begin *any* day.

I can always face January with optimism. After all, it's the traditional time for a new start . . . a fresh beginning . . . a clean, blank page.

But Samuel Johnson's prayer caused me to stop, ponder, and personalize that prayer. I have found myself reading and then re-reading it. Many phrases have challenged me.

One phrase especially has already etched itself upon my memory:

> ". . . *and grant that the time which Thou shalt yet*
> *allow me may not pass unprofitably away."*

The Apostle Paul expressed the same idea in saying that he did not want to "live in vain." He did not want to serve spuriously and then become a "castaway."

All about us are wasted lives . . . misspent lives. We who are servants often find ourselves called upon to bind the bruised, mend the broken, and salvage the remains of "what could have been."

But what of ourselves? It takes high resolve to stay on course. It takes discipline, perseverance, a steadied focus, and a prayerful daily journey to keep from living unprofitably. Let's pray for each other in this regard.

I urge you to read Samuel Johnson's prayer again and again. Read it slowly . . . thoughtfully . . . prayerfully. I have just taken a moment to pray for each reader of this book. May this be your best year in growth and ministry. It can be.

> *"Commit thy works unto the Lord, and thy thoughts*
> *shall be established."*   Proverbs 16:3 (KJV)

14

LORD, IS THIS FAIR?

I often need to be reminded that God is sovereign, not only in history but also in my life. Not just in the big things but also in the little things.

The trouble is, there's enough humanity in all of us to often feel sorry for ourselves. Too quickly we tend to compare ourselves with each other. This always leads to problems. Sooner or later, we usually end up crying out to God, "Lord, is this fair?"

"Lord, is it fair . . .
- that John has so many spiritual gifts and I have so few?"
- that Barbara gets all the breaks and I am overlooked?"
- that Mark and Fran are always so good, accurate and effective at what they do and I seem to be so slow and ineffective?"
- that Jeff gets all the conveniences of city life and I am stuck out here in the jungle?" (vice versa)
- that Louis and Eve have such public ministries with large results and we labor unnoticed and unappreciated?"

At such times we need to get back into the Word, specifically 1 Corinthians 12:4-6 (NASB), which reminds us that God is sovereign in the entire process of ministry. The text says (1) *there are a variety of gifts* (several dozen of them are mentioned in the epistles); (2) *a variety of ministries* (that is, a variety of spheres and arenas for ministry); and (3) *a variety of effects* (meaning that there are differences of results, large and small).

God, in His all-wise sovereignty, makes the choices as to your gifts, your area of assignment, and the results of your ministry. Remember these phrases in 1 Corinthians 12:

15

> The Spirit distributes to each one individually **just as He wills**. (vs. 11)

> God has placed the members, each of them, in the body, **just as He desired**. (vs. 18)

When I accept God's sovereignty in everything related to my ministry, it ought to eliminate three ugly sins that habitually threaten to discourage me . . . envy, pride, and self-pity. Think about it--if God is really sovereign, is there any room for these debilitating sins?

Well, God *is* sovereign. It is *His choice* as to the place He wants you to have in His worldwide ministry. Hear it again . . . **It is His choice.**

But it is *your* choice . . . it is *my* choice . . .
    - TO BE AVAILABLE TO HIM
    - TO BE FAITHFUL TO HIM
    - TO BE GRATEFUL TO HIM

> *" . . . godliness with contentment is great gain."*
>   1 Timothy 6:6 (NIV)

16

THE LASTING POWER OF EASTER

As I pen this letter to you, it is late Easter Sunday night. It has been a good day . . . warm and sunny . . . time with the family . . . inspiring worship services with enthusiastic singing . . . reverent reflections on the timeless message of Christ's resurrection.

But in a few minutes, it will no longer be Easter. In fact, by the time you read this, the Easter celebration of this year will be history. So why am I writing to you about Easter?

The answer is found in Ephesians 1:19-20. Paul prays that Christians would grasp and use this "incomparably great power" which is the same "mighty strength, which [God] exerted in Christ when he raised him from the dead" (NIV). Those powerful words tell me that every day is Easter for the Christian. Today. Tomorrow. Every day.

Resurrection power is available to me now in my life and ministry. And this same power, Resurrection Power, is for your use right now . . .

> **Resurrection Power** to lift you from despair.
> **Resurrection Power** to give you victory over sin.
> **Resurrection Power** to assure you of God's forgiveness.
> **Resurrection Power** to steady you in tough times.
> **Resurrection Power** to enjoy God's real presence.
> **Resurrection Power** to cover regrets from your past.
> **Resurrection Power** to prosper your ministry.

Why is it that we so quickly forget the Easter message? Too easily we slip into old ruts of trusting human resources instead of Resurrection Power.

Jesus, who said, *"I was dead but I am alive forever and ever"* (Revelation 1:18, NIV), lives in you and me to quicken us . . . to enable us . . . to empower us. Do we really *believe* it?

This is the year-round message of Easter--that every day is Easter day. Allow this risen Christ to touch you with His Power *today.*

> *"I have been crucified with Christ and I no longer live, but Christ lives in me. The life I live in the body, I live by faith in the Son of God, who loved me and gave himself for me."*
>
> Galatians 2:20 (NIV)

INVINCIBLE FAITH

Some 2,000 years ago Jesus said, "I will build my Church and the gates of hell shall not prevail against it" (Matthew 16:18, KJV). The word "prevail" is translated variously: "overpower" (NASB), and "overthrow" (WILLIAMS). Jesus made it convincingly clear. He would build the church and nothing . . . say it again, *NOTHING* could stop Him.

Today He is still building His Church. Indeed, His Church has been often opposed . . . and persecuted . . . and hindered . . . and threatened. Yet, the Church continues to grow. In fact, missiologists give us the fact that about 60,000 individuals are being added *every day* to the Church worldwide.

I have seen this reality of church growth. I saw it in the mountains of Ecuador as we worshiped with the Colorado Indians. I saw it in Egypt as I preached to hundreds of Christians, including four with

18

Islamic backgrounds who had committed their lives to Christ and were imprisoned because of their faith and Christian commitment. I saw it in Hong Kong where I preached to a small congregation of forty believers who had been meeting together for worship for just six months.

All over the world, the Lord Jesus is building His Church.

When my wife, Evie, and I recently visited China, we spent thirteen days there visiting with pastors and seminary leaders. We were amazed at what we discovered. But first, let me remind you of recent Chinese history:

- In 1949, all missionaries were forced out of China when the Communists took over the government.

- In 1966, during the cultural revolution, church buildings were closed. Many of them became schools, factories, apartments, even machine shops. Pastors were either placed on farms or sent to work in factories. I met several who had done both when their churches were taken from them.

It appeared to many that Christianity was dead and buried in China in 1966.

For the next twelve to fifteen years, there was little communication either in or out of China. For all we knew, the flickering flame of Christian faith had been extinguished. But we learned that indeed the Church in China was not dead . . . but alive and doing very well. God had been building the Church, even without missionaries . . . even with the church buildings closed . . . even with pastors "out of their pulpits."

That's why the story of the Church in China today is so exciting. In September 1979, the government allowed churches to reopen. Today there are 4,000 reopened churches. There are another 10,000 to 20,000 house churches.

Whereas there were some 700,000 Christians in China in 1949, today there are an estimated five million, acknowledged by the government. However, other estimates are as high as *50 million* believers! Ten seminaries have been reopened. Every month, 45 new churches are reopening!

We visited with many Christians in China who asked for prayer and their requests were most specific. I share them here with you:

~Pray that doors will continue to open.

~Pray that government policies will continue to be friendly to the church.

~Pray that pastors and church leaders can receive adequate training to lead the church.

~Pray for maturity among the believers.

~Pray that a "Billy Graham" might arise from within the Chinese community.

Yes, Jesus is building His Church, so please remember you are on the *winning team.* Your part in His ministry is an eternal investment. The Lord is building His Church *through you.* Hang in there!

> *"Be strong and take heart, all you who hope in the Lord."*
> Psalm 31:24 (NIV)

DANGERS FOR WORD SPECIALISTS

"Let the Word of Christ dwell in you richly as you teach and admonish one another with all wisdom, and as you sing psalms, hymns, and spiritual songs."

Colossians 3:16 (NIV)

Many of us in Christian ministry are called also to be WORD-SPECIALISTS. That is, we may function as teachers, preachers, professors, or translators of the Word. What a great privilege. But in the text above, every Christian is urged to be a WORD-CARRIER. And that's an equally special privilege.

In my case, I chose the ministry because of a great love for the Word of God, instilled in me while yet a child. After college, I spent three years in seminary to become proficient in the Word, and later, a doctorate further equipped me to know and preach the Word with clarity and excellence. And, during these past years, I have often spent 25 hours each week studying the Word in the preparation of sermons. Again, it's a great privilege.

Yet, I have discovered some subtle built-in dangers in being a WORD-SPECIALIST. After pouring over the Scriptures for hours, weeks, months, and years, I've often noticed something negative happened in my relationship to these Scriptures. I developed a detached over-familiarity with the Scriptures and I approached the Book with only a professional or vocational interest. Have you ever had that experience?

Once we approached the Book as eager children, reading God's "love letter" to us. We were loving servants waiting and listening to hear the Master's voice.

But now, perhaps, we come simply and routinely to the Word . . . to translate another paragraph . . . to prepare a Bible lesson . . . to make another sermon. If we were to stop and think about it, we'd see that we do not come for personal feeding . . . for spiritual nourishment . . . for edification and blessing. We come just out of habit or routine.

In fact, it's possible to produce excellent sermons that are properly exegeted, graphically illustrated, and eloquently delivered and yet be personally unaffected by the Word. It is also possible to do an excellent translation of the Word into a distant mother tongue and yet be spiritually impoverished ourselves.

Congregations run the same risk. Kierkegaard once warned congregations to beware of merely being "sermon tasters" (sermon evaluators).

The purpose of God's Word in us is *to change us* as we embrace the truth with a commitment to obedience. The Apostle James put it this way: *"Be doers of the Word"* (James 1:22, KJV).

Do you, too, sometimes need this reminder? Love the Book. Live the Book . . . and let those basic commitments to the Word bring a positive impact to your teaching, preaching, and translating of this great Book.

> *"But as for you, continue in what you have learned and have become convinced of, because you know those from whom you learned it, and how from infancy you have known the Holy Scriptures, which are able to make you wise for salvation through faith in Christ Jesus."*
>
> 2 Timothy 3: 14-15 (NIV)

TRICK QUESTIONS AND NICKNAMES

Have you ever heard of "Joseph, the Levite from Cyprus"?

That's not meant to be a trick question. Undoubtedly you know him. But maybe you know him better by his nickname, Barnabas, as explained in Acts 4:36 . . . *"there was a man named Joseph, a Levite from Cyprus, whom the apostles called Barnabas (which means Son of Encouragement)."*

This unusual man is called Joseph only once in the New Testament. Generally (in Acts, chapters 4,9,11-15), he is called by his new name, *"the Encourager."* Barnabas was given his nickname because he really was a *"lifestyle encourager."* When you follow him around in the Book of Acts, he is *always* living up to this title given to him.

Barnabas was an ENCOURAGING PASTOR. His ministry in Antioch was positive, uplifting, and edifying. The impact on his congregation was buoyant as he "encouraged them all to remain true to the Lord with all their hearts" (Acts 11:23, NIV). Barnabas was a positive model to his church flock. He had an impact on them for goodness and joyfulness.

Barnabas was also an ENCOURAGING PREACHER. He powerfully explained the Scriptures as he traveled as part of his itinerant ministry. There are sixteen references to Barnabas' use of the Scriptures in his preaching. He knew that the eternal Word of God was the greatest source of real encouragement. We cannot improve on that finding. That continues to be true.

Apart from his role as pastor and preacher, Barnabas was an ENCOURAGING FRIEND. He took time for one-on-one relationships with people. Several of those relationships were redemptive and life-changing:

- Barnabas believed in Paul, when the rest of the apostles rejected Paul as not genuinely converted. Paul was renewed and spiritually vitalized by this friendship.

- Barnabas accepted John Mark and gave him a "second chance" opportunity for ministry even after Mark had "dropped out" earlier.

In both cases the friendship of Barnabas to these men was used by God to totally transform and tutor these men into effective servants for God. Although those around Paul and Mark had little confidence in their potential for ministry, Barnabas convinced the critics to give the men a chance to prove themselves with God's help. And they did!

Barnabas was an ENCOURAGING MISSIONARY. Actually, he was a cross-cultural missionary. Barnabas was always a welcome sight as he *"strengthened and encouraged Christians to remain true to the faith"* (Acts 14:22). As Barnabas traveled from city to city, this mighty missionary was God's special channel of *hope and encouragement*.

God is calling all of us Christians to take on this nickname--to be encouragers. In fact, we are exhorted frequently *"to encourage one another"* (Hebrews 3:13, 10:25; 1 Thessalonians 4:18, 5:11).

The ministry of encouragement is not optional. It is not supplemental. It is not peripheral. *It is central to your total life of ministry.* And . . . without it, your ministry will have little lasting impact . . . little life-transforming power . . . little real help to people.

Many of those who deal with contemporary problems and psychological difficulties know how shattered self-esteem, abuse, or dysfunctional relationships can cripple and maim personalities and spirits. Our generation sorely needs encouragers . . . in the home, in the church, on the mission station. God's desire is that His children be "greatly encouraged" (Hebrews 6:18). *That encouragement could come through you.*

> *"We ask you, fellow Christians, to appreciate the men who work with you and lead you in the Lord and warn you. Love them and think very highly of them on account of the work they're doing."*
>
> 1 Thessalonians 5:12-13 (Beck)

THROUGH DARK TUNNELS

J.B. Phillips said it in such a way that I have never forgotten it . . . "Sooner or later, we will all travel through a dark tunnel." Our experiences in the dark tunnels are always memorable, and I suppose that this writing of author J.B. Phillips is an unforgettable phrase for several reasons:

~*Because the Bible affirms this to be truth.* Jesus said, "In the world you will have trouble" (John 16:33). Other Biblical writers state and rephrase the same reality.

~*Because the experience of humanity confirms the same.* As a pastoral counselor, I have often talked with parishioners, friends, and occasionally with total strangers through their personal difficult and varied "tunnel times."

25

~Because my personal experience verifies the principle.
I, too, have traveled through some terrifying dark tunnels.

So have you . . . in the past . . . and maybe even right now.

Or, perhaps they lie ahead in your future.

Often these tunnels are so dark . . . without a hint of light. Scary, too . . . and lonely. And sometimes the darkness has stubbornly persisted while I cried out to the Lord, "Will this darkness ever leave me?" We wonder if we can ever escape from the dark tunnel.

There is a good word from the Lord for such times. Theologians call it "omnipresence." This means that the Lord is always present. Again, He is *always present with us . . . He is always with you.*

HE IS WITH YOU just as He was with the initial band of disciple/missionaries in Matthew 28. He not only commissioned them and sent them out, He also gave them a promise, stated in Matthew 28:20: "I am with you *always.*" Every missionary needs to affirm that truth often . . . for life and for ministry.

HE IS WITH YOU in the "fiery experiences of life." When King Nebuchadnezzar looked into the terrible furnace to see if he had destroyed Shadrach, Meshach, and Abednego, he saw a fourth person, looking like a "son of the gods" (Daniel 3:25). Jesus was with His people in the fiery furnace. So, I can be confident that in every private furnace . . . in every personal tunnel, Jesus will also be with you. Whether it be the furnace of illness or persecution . . . whether it be the dark tunnel of family crisis or tragedy, He will be there. In fact, in "whatsoever" circumstances you find yourself, *He is there* with you. You are never alone.

HE IS WITH YOU, too, at that fearful and lonely time when you or your loved one must walk through life's corridor to physical death.

David, with great confidence, stated, *"When I walk through the valley of the shadow of death . . . God will be with me"* (Psalm 23:4).

Be prepared for the reality of dark tunnels . . . fiery furnaces. But also be prepared for the presence of God. You will always have a FRIEND . . . a COMPANION . . . because the EVER-PRESENT GOD will be with you.

> *"I have told you these things, so that in me you may have peace. In this world you will have trouble. But take heart! I have overcome the world."*
> John 16:33 (NIV)

McPRAYERS

I've been worrying lately that my prayers are too routine and similar to fast-food fare . . . quick and easy, but lacking in true substance. The writer Berridge once stated, "All decay begins in the closet. No heart thrives without much secret converse with God and nothing will make amends for the want of it." I agree with Berridge. I also agree with his comment that *nothing* can make up for the lack of prayer in our lives.

In recent months, God has been nudging me toward a greater personal commitment to prayer, especially the ministry of intercession. James 5:16 calls us to this ministry of *praying for one another*.

I certainly do affirm the need for more prayer. Yet, I find it difficult to always follow in that direction. Like you, no doubt, my prayer life has had its ups and downs. I have seen good days and "not so good" days, as far as a disciplined prayer commitment is concerned. In looking back on the times of my own neglected prayer, I clearly see now that such times were marked by devotional dryness . . . decreased spiritual vitality . . . lessened personal blessing . . . and degrees of ineffectiveness in ministry.

All Christians must pray. Of course, it's easy for us to believe in an imperative for great Christian leaders to be men and women of intercessory prayer. But maybe we aren't as quick to sense that need in our own lives and experiences. Yet the Bible explicitly states that we should intercede for fellow Christians, for Christian leaders, for world leaders, for strangers, for family members, for the nations of the world, for enemies, for the unsaved, and for more workers in Christian ministry. That's quite a list! I don't know of any category that was missed.

Indeed prayer was prominent in the personal life of Christ. It was also strategically important in the life of early church members and evident in the ministries of the first-century Christian leaders. They said, "We will give ourselves to prayer," as they sifted through the multiplicity of things that they were involving themselves with. **They adjusted their schedules** to make room for prayer. Is it time that we do the same?

Will you join me in making a new commitment to the priority of prayer? Especially, I invite you to join me in a worldwide movement of intercession. You will find, as I have, that this is a difficult commitment to keep. Satan will oppose you . . . the world will try to squeeze it out of your schedule . . . and the flesh will balk. Often, you and I will simply not *feel* like praying. But, let's keep on praying.

Let's intercede in the spare moments that we have. Let's also intercede in designated "block periods" in the daily schedule. Let's also occasionally spend prolonged fellowship in a personal prayer retreat. I have found such times to be especially precious. Intercessory prayer is a "win-win" situation. Both the subject of our prayers and we, ourselves, benefit greatly.

Our Heavenly Father says, "Come . . . come boldly into my Presence."

> *"The Lord is near to all who call on him, to all who call on him in truth. He fulfills the desires of those who fear him; he hears their cries and saves them."*
> Psalm 145: 18-19 (NIV)

SOME THOUGHTS ON FACING DEATH

It was 1:00 o'clock on a beautiful, sunny Saturday afternoon, and I was on a flight from Orlando, Florida to Chicago . . . and then on to our home in Rockford.

As I traveled that day, I was a grateful man . . . *profoundly* grateful. The past 36 hours had been a rollercoaster experience for me . . . emotionally, physically, and even spiritually.

Early in the morning of the day before my flight, I was awakened with intense chest pain. I called the hotel desk and in a matter of moments, a rapid, incredible series of events took place . . . a fast ride to the hospital by ambulance . . . nine hours in the emergency room hooked to IV feeding, heart monitor, and oxygen . . . numerous exams by several teams of physicians . . . blood test . . . several series of EKG's . . . chest x-rays, plus more tests.

The doctors told me that I was a very sick man and that I should expect a somewhat lengthy hospital stay. I couldn't believe it. I mean, *it did not seem real.* Just hours before, I was a picture of health and vitality. Then, abruptly, I was admitted to the Cardiac Care Unit, flat on my back in the midst of all the medical equipment and hospital personnel.

As I considered the apparent severity of my condition, a jumble of thoughts came over me. Strangely, there were no feelings of panic, fear, or terror. But, overwhelming thoughts of regret filled my mind . . . sorrow that perhaps my life would soon be over.

Had I preached my last sermon . . .
had I seen my family for the last time . . .
had I spoken my last word of
encouragement?

I remember thinking of the many things that I still hoped to do for people . . . and there was more to be done for the Lord.

The next twelve hours were filled with these lingering thoughts of sorrow and regret. Multiple tests continued all day.

That evening, doctors came to my room and said, "Mr. Lindquist, you have surprised us today. Instead of worsening, you have obviously improved. In fact, the tests indicate that you have not had a heart attack as we first suspected. We can't find anything wrong with you. You appear healthy . . . normal . . . and you can go home in the morning."

The doctors said I possibly had slight pericarditis but it was not serious, so they could treat me with drugs the next week at home.

Yes, I was both surprised and relieved to be released the next morning. In those 36 hours, I went from health to apparent loss of health and even fear for my life . . . back to a renewed evidence of good health. And during those 36 hours, the Prayer Chain in Rockford had hundreds of Christians praying. Also, 400 world Christian leaders in Orlando had prayed for me . . . *And God answered and delivered me!* Ironically, the time in the hospital was well spent . . . in reflection, recommitment, gratitude, and a special awareness of His *presence* and *power*.

> *"Consider it pure joy, my brothers, whenever you face trials of many kinds, because you know that the testing of your faith develops perseverance. Perseverance must finish its work so that you may be mature and complete, not lacking anything."*
>
> James 1:2-4 (NIV)

MANGER REFLECTIONS

A phrase from a familiar Christmas carol has persistently been on my mind in the past few weeks . . . "O come let us adore Him." I often catch myself humming it as I drive, even singing the verses aloud.

The phrase, of course, is reminiscent of the text in Matthew 2:11 which describes the visit of the wise men to the infant Lord Jesus.

It says that when they saw Him, "they fell down and worshiped Him."

The late A. W. Tozer called worship "the missing jewel" in describing the evangelical church of his generation. If this was an accurate assessment of the church in the Fifties, it is even more descriptive of the church of the Nineties.

Indeed, most of us know very little about WORSHIP . . . about ADORATION. Both publicly and privately, many of us are "kindergartners" in our understanding and practice. Often we are just not willing to take the time nor the necessary exercise for the discipline of true worship.

We try to meet God in the rush, instead of speaking to Him in the hush. We are content to know *about* Him without really *knowing Him*. We take a quick glance into His face, but know little of a steadied, unhurried gaze into the beautiful face of the Lord.

And . . . we are the poorer for our neglect of WORSHIP and ADORATION.

All of us in Christian ministry are busy people. We experience constant time-pressured personal demands placed on us by others. Or sometimes they are self-imposed. We so desperately need to step back and take a look at priorities. We need to slow down now and then. There needs to be some time *daily* for a quiet meeting with the Lord. Occasionally there also needs to be a prolonged and protracted period alone with Him.

God said to Isaiah, "Be still . . . and know that I am God."

Jesus said to His followers, "Come apart and rest a while."

God wants to meet you and me. When you are willing, He will give you His full undivided attention.   He has all the time in the world for private meetings with you and me.

When we *worship* God, we attribute worth to Him . . . we focus on His great and glorious attributes. And like worship, adoration is a deliberate persistent, uninterrupted focus upon the Lord Himself. It is a focus on Him . . . not only His attributes . . . on His nature . . . on His promises . . . on His resources . . . on His names.

Often I find that it is helpful to have my Bible open at such times. I also enjoy the hymn book as an aid in ADORATION. Above all, I need blocks of designated time for personal WORSHIP AND ADORATION.

Perhaps this could be the time when you discover or rediscover the magnificence of ADORATION as did the wise men so long ago. I pray that your discovery will be marked by new dimensions of WORSHIP AND ADORATION.

> *"Blessed are those who have learned to acclaim You, who walk in the light of Your presence, O Lord. They rejoice in Your name all day long; they exalt in Your righteousness."*
>
> Psalm 89:15-16 (NIV)

SHORT SPEECHES
AND LONG-TERM GOALS

In the later years of his life, Winston Churchill made a visit to his childhood school. The appearance was preannounced, and everyone was expecting the British statesman to make a speech. Enthusiasm was high. Expectation was great. The moment finally came for Churchill to rise to the podium. His speech was short . . . unusually short. In fact, here is the speech in its entirety:

"Never . . . never . . . never . . . never give up!"

Our generation needs to embrace the message of that speech. Too often we Christians are negatively intimidated and subdued by the spirit and culture of our time. Surrounded by fast foods, instant photos, and constant demands for immediate gratification, we find it difficult to have deep roots and long-term goals.

The New Testament frequently uses a Greek word, "*Hupomone.*" The verbal form of this word is "to remain, to persevere, and to endure." The noun synonyms are, "constancy, steadfastness, endurance, patience and perseverance."

My wife, Evie, and I recently returned from a visit to a mission station located in the jungles of Peru. Many of these exemplary Christians modeled *hupomone* in their lives and service.

I think, for example, of Scottie and Marie who have spent more than 25 years living in the jungle, working on a translation of the Scriptures. Often they have been buffeted by ill health and sometimes by discouragement. They worked *eight years* before anyone was converted to Christianity and even longer before the village chief finally came to Christ. But at that point, many other villagers were won to the Lord. Yet, Scottie and Marie waited *22 years* to see the mighty movement of God.

I think that most of us would have given up more quickly and gone home, falsely assuming that these tough times meant closed doors.

V. Raymond Edman, past president of Wheaton College, used to say, "It's always too soon to quit." Good advice!

We met a sharp young man, who had just returned from an uncertain trip to potentially dangerous areas. He privately confided to me, "I knew there was the possibility that my trip might be a one-way journey--that maybe I wouldn't return alive!"

I asked him how he felt about that possibility, and he replied, "I settled those questions before I came to South America. God's will is good . . . perfect." I'll never forget that look of steady faith and endurance in his eyes. Perseverance.

Perhaps you, too, need to be encouraged to persevere . . . to be steadfast. Results might be slow . . . health might be difficult . . . terrorism or violence might be a threat. But *persevere.*

Thank God for your life commitment, even when the journey is less than easy. Jesus is the model here for our faith. He endured much abuse but He never lost sight of the larger, long-term goal.

> *"Let us fix our eyes on Jesus, the author and perfecter of our faith, who for the joy set before him endured the cross, scorning its shame, and sat down at the right hand of the throne of God. Consider him who endured such opposition from sinful men, so that you will not grow weary and lose heart."*
> Hebrews 12:2-3 (NIV)

OVERWHELMING VICTORY

In 1988, Evie and I made a visit to the childhood home of Corrie ten Boom, located in the downtown section of Haarlem, the Netherlands. We were surprised to see that nearly a half-century later, it again houses a clock shop on the first floor. The upper floors have been restored to living quarters, as similar as possible to the days of the ten Boom occupancy. The top floor is now a museum, telling the story of this brave family who hid Jews in their "hiding place," accessible through the bottom shelf of the linen closet in Corrie's tiny bedroom.

Eventually the ten Boom family was sent to concentration camps, where most of them died.

As we stood in the small rooms and observed the surroundings, I was deeply moved by a wall motto in their living room. The inscription was short and in Dutch . . . "JEZUS, DE OVERWINNAAR." In English, that phrase declares the truth that Jesus is the OverWinner, the Conqueror, the Triumphant One.

Corrie ten Boom grew up as a girl seeing that motto on the wall. The message of the motto then became a conviction of her heart. Its truth shaped her courage. Later, when she was in the concentration camps as a prisoner, the wall motto's truth brought hope to her heart.

As an older woman after release from the prison, Corrie traveled the world telling the story of the sufficiency and reality of Christ to her and her family. The message of "The Hiding Place," whether the book or film, dramatizes the real life story of one family that believed that Jesus is indeed the Conqueror in every situation.

Because Jesus is the OverWinner, *we* can also be OverWinners. That is the message of Romans 8:35 which catalogs problems like

36

"trouble, hardship, persecution, famine, nakedness, danger and sword." Then the Apostle sums it all up in Romans 8:37: "in all these things we are more than conquerors through Christ."

Did you catch that, "We are more than conquerors *through Christ*." That is the pivotal phrase. We are winners *through Him*. In ourselves, we cannot make it. In and of ourselves we are losers, not winners. We are victims, not victors. But . . . in Christ, we can be winners.

Corrie ten Boom's little motto is more than a nice phrase or glib platitude. It is living Christian truth . . . objective truth translated into life. Because He is the Victorious One, you really also can be victorious . . . IN EVERY SITUATION.

Every situation? Yes! Even when temptation strongly gnaws away at your resolve . . . when trials weigh you down heavily . . . when your task seems so large and you feel so inadequate . . . when sorrow sweeps over you . . . when mediocrity has settled in and you have bypassed the highest possibilities . . . when loneliness leaves you cold and scared . . . *every situation.*

Corrie's older sister, Betsy, while still in the concentration camp, wrote, "There is no pit so deep but that God is deeper yet."

> *"But in all these things we overwhelmingly conquer through Him who loved us."*
> Romans 8:37 (NASB)

GOD'S GLASNOST

I received an incredibly encouraging letter from a single young man living in the Soviet Union, written in very good English. I must share segments of the letter with you . . . but first, some background.

I was with the John Guest team for meetings in several cities in the Soviet Union. One afternoon we had a sound stage set up on Arbat Street, the popular pedestrian street in Moscow. We had a marathon service in the open air with several of us pastors and musicians sharing Christ. Hundreds listened and remained to talk with us. After I preached, Mike (not his real name) came to me and wanted to talk. He had never heard the Gospel before. He liked what he heard but wasn't ready to make a commitment. However, he did ask if I'd correspond with him to help him with his English. I offered to do two things: to send him our monthly letter of *Encouragement* and to answer any letter that he wrote me. I heard nothing until two weeks ago. Enjoy the following excerpts:

"Although I've very small hope my letter will ever get to you (in spite of all this perestroika and glasnost stuff, letters keep on vanishing quite mysteriously), I'm determined to give it a try. I want you to know how I appreciate your sending me these ENCOURAGEMENT letters. . . . I really didn't know what to make of it. A person I scarcely knew has taken an effort to send me a message on a subject that had nothing to do with everyday life. That was how I felt about it. Come to think of it, it was an unheard of thing in a country like modern Russia. Everyone's busy fighting for survival, chasing things of no spirit value; moral inhibitions being a thing of a long past. And then there was your second letter. The moment I've spotted the familiar envelope in my mailbox I realized I've been waiting subconsciously for it all that time. Until that day the very idea of God's love has been just another abstract thought to me. Your letters made me wonder what power urges you to send a kind word to another human being. And then everything fell in place. I also discovered what I needed badly was a visual image and here the film "JESUS" came to us. It has been a great help. Now that I've got that feeling that I'm not alone in this world . . . that there's Someone who cares, I won't part with it for all the money in the world."

I share this letter with you for several reasons. First, I hope it encourages you to see God at work in Eastern Europe . . . one of many stories of hope after decades of darkness.

Secondly, pray that Christians will learn how to maximize this hour of openness. None of us knows how long it will last.

Thirdly, "Mike's" story is an illustration of seedtime and harvest. Earlier, a seed was planted. Others have watered. God, in His own timing, has brought life and light. Let's keep spreading the seed. Let's not be deterred whether or not we see immediate results.

> Give as 'twas given to you in your need,
> Love as the Master loved you;
> Be to the helpless a helper indeed,
> Unto your mission be true.
>
> (Refrain)
> Make me a blessing, Make me a blessing,
> Out of my life may Jesus shine.
> Make me a blessing, O Saviour I pray,
> Make me a blessing to someone today.
> —Ira B. Wilson

LOOKING OUT FOR NUMBER ONE

One of America's favorite hymns is "HOW GREAT THOU ART," which is also loved around this world. I have heard this hymn sung not only in English, but in other languages, including Melanesian Pidgin, "TOK PISIN" (the trade language of Papua New Guinea).

The chorus says . . . "How great Thou art, How great Thou art." I especially like the way that phrase is expressed in Melanesian Pidgin . . . *Yu Nambawan, Yu Wanpela, Yu Bikpela.*

A literal transliteration of these words back into English would read: "You are Number One, You are the First One, You are the Great One." I really like that.

In English, of course, the hymn makes a general theological statement about God's Greatness. But in Pidgin, the hymn makes a very *personal* statement about God's Greatness. It speaks of the vital Christian life expressed in personal Lordship . . . the believer in submission to the Sovereign Lord.

A few years ago, one of America's best-selling books was *Looking Out for Number One.* It brashly challenged the reader to embrace selfishness as a driving force in life. It picked up on the egocentric mood of the 1970's and tried to legitimize it as acceptable.

In striking contrast to that selfish approach to life, the Christian is called . . . not to serve self, but Christ . . . not to seek self-glory, but God's Glory . . . *not to live for **me**, but for **Him**.*

The issue is *Lordship.* Campus Crusade for Christ has challenged those of us who are Christians to examine our lives to see . . . "who is on the Throne?" There is a continual daily struggle over this issue. Am I trying to be in control? Or, am I consciously submitting to His leadership?

40

None of us easily or readily submits to the Lordship of Christ. Nor do we usually settle this matter once for all. It is a daily matter--and often a *many times daily* matter--of deliberately inviting Christ to control us. Not just in the big issues, but in *all* issues: how we use our time . . . how we spend our finances . . . friendships . . . relationships . . . priorities . . . pleasures . . . *everything*.

Paul brings us to the heart of Lordship in Colossians 1:18:
"Make Jesus pre-eminent in everything."

It was J. Stewart Holden who once wrote:
"Christ does not want a place in your life.
He does not even want prominence in your life.
He demands pre-eminence."

As Christ's servants, let's not fool ourselves about Lordship. Just because we are involved in ministry does not necessarily mean that we have recognized His Lordship in all of life. And Lordship in some areas does not automatically indicate Lordship in all areas.

Let's join our Christian friends in Papua New Guinea in singing to our Lord, *Yu Nambawan, Yu Wanpela, Yu Bikpela* . . . You are Number One . . . You are the First One . . . You are the Great One. Better yet, let's live it out in our lives.

> *"The one who sows to please his sinful nature, from that nature will reap destruction; the one who sows to please the Spirit, from the Spirit will reap eternal life."*
> Galatians 6:8 (NIV)

THE ENCOURAGER'S PRAYER

In 1988, my wife, Evie, a friend, and I were about half finished with a two-month ministry tour of four countries in Asia. As we ministered to missionaries, national church leaders, and some of the other Christians, we often found ourselves asking God, "Lord, make us encouragers."

I, from this, put some prayer thoughts on paper and called it *The Encourager's Prayer.* I hope that it will inspire you today:

Lord, as I come into your presence today, I recognize that You are called the Great Encourager in the Scriptures. I read that Jesus, too, is referred to as an Encourager. I further see that the Holy Spirit is known as the Paraclete, often translated . . . "Encourager, Helper or literally . . . the One who comes alongside of me."

Thank you, Lord, for Your constant ministry of Encouragement displayed all through the Bible . . .

- *When Elijah was discouraged in ministry, You encouraged and refreshed him.*
- *When David was misunderstood, hated and maligned, You manifested Yourself to him and he was encouraged.*
- *When Timothy was fearful and insecure, You steadied and affirmed him.*
- *When Peter denied you and tearfully repented, You accepted him and forgave him.*
- *When the woman at the well shared her loneliness and emptiness, You gave her purpose and direction.*
- *When Matthew (with a less than exemplary past) offered himself to You for ministry, You welcomed him and gave him a new start.*

Lord, what an Encourager you have been to these friends from the past. And You have been an Encourager to me. Thank you, too, for all the people You have sent along to be Your messengers of encouragement to me. I can see that these human instruments have been sovereignly appointed by You . . . well chosen, well placed, and well-timed. Thank you.

And now, what shall I ask? Just one thing. Lord, please make me an encourager. I read in Your Word that all of Your children are to be encouragers. What an honor. I am amazed that You could use me as Your channel of encouragement.

Who am I that I could ever bless and encourage another pilgrim along the way. But I am willing. And I remind You today that I am available.

Too often I have not been an encourager. I'm afraid that instead of lightening the load of others, sometimes I have made their loads heavier. Instead of bringing hope and cheer, I have insensitively been occupied with my own concerns and agendas. I confess this as sin.

I commit myself to You for this ministry of encouragement. I ask that You will help me to creatively, spontaneously, and sensitively look for opportunities. I ask, further, that this ministry of encouragement will not be occasional . . . but that it will become my lifestyle . . . a "way of life" for me.

Lord, I know that I cannot do this by myself. So please live in me . . . love through me . . . lift Your servants through me . . . and bless others through me. Make me Your messenger of encouragement today. Amen.

Will you keep this prayer before you as you go about the Father's business in the coming days? Everyone around you needs an inspiring word . . . a positive encouragement in the Lord.

> *"A man's spirit sustains him in sickness, but a crushed spirit who can bear?"*
>
> Proverbs 13:14 (NIV)

> *". . . a word spoken in due season, how good is it!"*
>
> Proverbs 15:23 (NIV)

FLAWED WORKS

Agra, India is best known for its magnificent Taj Mahal. As soon as you see it, you know why it is one of the Seven Wonders of the World . . . one of the great architectural masterpieces of all time. Massive, yet exquisite. Built of brilliant white marble and embedded with precious and semiprecious stones, the Taj Mahal is absolutely awesome from a distance yet even more overwhelming and beautiful when examined at close range.

There is, however, another great edifice being built now in Agra. Some say it will be even more resplendent than the Taj Mahal. It is the Radhasoami Temple, a worship center based on the teaching of its founder, Soamiji Maharaj. The religion started in 1861. The temple's construction began in 1904. Work has continued for the last 90 years.

The expected date of completion of the Radhasoami Temple is not for fifty years or so. Can you imagine? Hundreds of craftsmen working daily on this great marble structure, as they have for nearly a century--and they are only about two-thirds finished. Sculptors spend months, even years, designing and sculpting flowers and leaves out of marble and then cutting jewels to be embedded in the marble. The only acceptable standard for the temple's construction is <u>excellence</u>.

Recently, I spent some time visiting Agra and specifically stopped to see this temple. I observed the craftsmen working on a rose about four inches in size--not much bigger than a real one--chiseled out of marble. As I watched, the artist made a mistake and flawed the marble. He immediately set it aside, rejected and useless. I asked if I could have the piece of flawed marble, and he gave it to me as a gift. Now I have it sitting in front of me on my desk as a reminder to always pursue excellence.

The Apostle Paul in Philippians 3 gave us a similar charge-- *"Approve excellence."*

In 1 Corinthians 3, Paul says that each of us Christians are builders. God has given us many opportunities and building materials. We are to build our personal lives, our ministries, and our families. Excellence is to characterize the entire building process . . .

    - excellence in choosing the best available materials;
    - excellence in using our best available skills;
    - excellence in using faithfulness and integrity in the
      details of our lives and ministries.

Paul says, *"Be careful how you build"* (3:10). He also says that someday *"the quality of our work will be tested"* (3:13), and further says that our work will be *"rewarded"* (3:14).

45

Our generation of Christian workers needs these reminders. Often we are so busy that sometimes the frantic speed of daily living squeezes out quality. Mediocrity becomes acceptable. Carelessness becomes the norm if we forget that our Heavenly Father is our Employer and will someday be our Rewarder.

The three wise men set the pattern by bringing "gold, frankincense and myrrh," the very best possible gifts to Jesus. Not trinkets or worthless junk, but *treasures*. Can we do less?

And so as I look at this marble rose on my desk, I see what started out as a lovely piece of sculpture. But it became flawed, rejected, and set aside as useless. And I do not want that to be me.

The lesson is clear. I must *pursue excellence*.

> *"Do your best to present yourself to God an approved workman who has nothing to be ashamed of . . ."*
> 2 Timothy 2:15 (WILLIAMS)

> *"Whatever you do, do it with all your heart, as work for the Lord and not for men . . ."*
> Colossians 3:23 (WILLIAMS)

GO FOR IT!

There are some prominent names in aviation history . . . you'd probably list the Wright brothers . . . then maybe Charles Lindbergh . . . and you might think of a man I met one day in 1988. Sitting across the aisle, flying home from Atlanta, was Dick Rutan.

Some years ago, Dick and his brother dreamed of building their own airplane with the capability of traveling around the world. They worked at the project despite discouraging comments like . . .

> "It will never work" . . .
> > "That's impossible" . . .
> > > "It's never been done before."

But Dick Rutan, his brother, and Dick's copilot persisted. They called their plane *Voyager*. Finally the aircraft was built, then tested. Dick Rutan and his copilot came to their scheduled day of departure. The trip was destined to be trouble-plagued right from the start . . . the tip of one of the wings broke off during take-off . . . they encountered vicious storms . . . they also had bouts with motion sickness. But, nine days after lift-off, the two returned, successfully completing their "impossible" mission.

I told Dick that my son, Reese, is a pilot and that he would appreciate an autograph. Dick Rutan then handed me the following note for my son. It read: "To Reese: DREAM . . . GO FOR IT." And he signed the note.

The message was brief . . . "DREAM . . . GO FOR IT." But I couldn't help thinking what a good message it was--especially for all of us involved in Christian ministry. The dual admonitions are these: Be a DREAMER and BE A DOER. Not one or the other, but both. We are to be DREAMERS THAT BECOME DOERS.

47

The Prophet Joel (2:28-32) said that in the last days there would be dreamers and visionaries and that they would come from the ranks of both young and old, of both men and women. I see that happening all over the world. People are catching the vision of ministry to people . . . the vision of their personal potential . . . the vision of usefulness in the hand of the Lord.

Often our dreams become smothered by our own feelings of inadequacy. And as if that weren't enough, we also get the message all too loudly and clearly from our detractors: "That's impossible" . . . "It'll never work" . . . "That's never been done before." Too long we have played all those *"I can't"* recordings in our minds. The Apostle Paul wrote of such a time in his life (Romans 7) but also wrote of reprogramming his mind which said, "I can!" In Philippians 4:13 he wrote, "*I can do all things through Christ* who strengthens me."

What is *your* dream? And how can it be discovered? There may be clues from looking at our backgrounds, our talents, our gifts, the perceived needs around us, and the open doors before us. Dreams also grow out of our personal walk with God. I am praying for you--
> ~ that your eyes will be open to the needs of others,
> ~ that your ears will hear the nudging of the Lord,
> ~ that your heart will be "in sync" with the Savior's heart.

Ann Kiemel often writes about dreams. Recently I heard her give this advice--which I find to be absolutely essential. Ann said, "Make Jesus the center of your dream." Again, Dick Rutan's words come back to me--"DREAM . . . GO FOR IT."

> *"But thanks be to God, which giveth us the victory through our Lord Jesus Christ."*
> 1 Corinthians 15:57 (NIV)

FORGOTTEN BY GOD?

Do you ever feel lonely? Have you ever felt *forgotten* by God? Abandoned? Deserted?

Surprisingly, *most* of God's saints can answer a resounding "*yes*" to this question. Perhaps David spoke for us all when he cried: *"How long, O Lord? Will you forget me forever?"* (Psalm 13:1, NIV).

David's feelings obscured the greater reality of the nature of God. In truth, God *will never forget* His children. In fact, God *cannot forget* us. The only thing He forgets is our sins, when they are confessed to Him. Beyond that, He has a flawless memory.

Hebrews 6:10 has often been an encouragement: *"God is not unjust; He will not forget your work and the love you have shown Him as you have helped His people and continue to help them."*

Notice that this verse mentions *three things God will never forget:*

1. HE WILL NEVER FORGET YOUR WORK. Perhaps your particular assignment is difficult . . . in a remote setting far from family and friends. Maybe your work is tedious, demanding, uncomfortable . . . even boring. But you are there because God sent you there. That has not gone unnoticed. God *has not* forgotten you or your work.

2. HE WILL NEVER FORGET YOUR LOVE FOR HIM. Hopefully, you're involved in ministry because of your love for the Lord. That's a powerful motivation. And it's this "*agape*" love--His unconditional love--that keeps us going.

   John Stott says, "The Christian life is essentially a love relationship." A retired preacher spoke to me when I was just a young preacher with this advice: "Love the Lord and

49

you will have a great ministry." But love tends to cool and deteriorate. It regularly needs to be stoked. Yes, the Lord will remember your love for Him. But you'll have to keep it alive by stirring up the coals from time to time.

3. HE WILL NEVER FORGET YOUR HELP TO THE SAINTS. The word translated "help" in this verse is literally "service." It's talking about people-ministry. Many Christian workers have shared frustration with me about the multiple interruptions and intrusions of people into their daily schedule. It is good to know that God knows all about these interruptions. He will remember every "cup of cold water" that you have given to others in His Name. So look for daily opportunities to give to this ministry.

Jesus promised to meet us at His Judgment with a "Well Done," and the old hymn says, "It will be worth it all when we see Jesus."

Even if it seems that you have been forgotten by friends and family, God *has not* and *never will forget you*. Your "work, love and helps to the saints" will be remembered and rewarded. It's all in the "Scroll of Remembrance" (Malachi 3:16), kept by His side.

> "When all my labors and trials are o'er
> And I am safe on that beautiful shore,
> Just to be near the dear Lord I adore
> Will through the ages be glory for me."
> --Charles H. Gabriel

". . . Continue to fight the good fight, by keeping your hold on faith and a good conscience . . ."
1 Timothy 1: 18,19 (Williams)

JUST JESUS

Several months ago, my friend Rich Gathro and I spent a couple of hours together with another friend, Doug Coe. We met in the office of Senate Chaplain Richard Halverson in Washington, D.C. The conversation was thoughtful . . . stimulating . . . even world encompassing, as we discussed effective means of representing Christ, especially in the difficult-to-reach areas of the world.

Doug has traveled and ministered in 196 countries. He has introduced many individuals to Christ. He is indeed a discipler . . . and an effective ambassador for Christ. Following our time together, I carried away one very strong impression that continues to affect my thinking of presenting Christ to the unconvinced and uncommitted masses around the world. Here it is. First of all, remember that EFFECTIVE EVANGELISM IS NOT:

- arguing religion with those from other belief systems;
- discussing merits and distinctives of denominationalism;
- talking about the church, whether local or universal;
- using trite cliches which are meaningless to people who do not know Christ;
- presenting Christianity only as a historical, ecclesiastical organized system. Historically, so much was done *negatively* in the Name of Christ that it erected walls between us and those we hope to influence.

EFFECTIVE EVANGELISM IS TALKING ABOUT JESUS. But, that's being overly simplistic, you say. Too simple? Too obvious? No, I think not. You see, the EFFECTIVE EVANGELIST is one who is involved in a significant relationship with Christ--loving Him, knowing Him, trusting Him, following Him, and sharing Him. Jesus is the heart of our message and it becomes an easy matter to talk about Him that way.

Remember when the Clinton administration was campaigning for the U.S. presidency? We were told that there was a sign on the wall of every office they used. It said, simply, "It's the economy, Stupid!" It was used to remind them to focus only on that simple issue and not try to argue other areas. In the same way we want to stay focused on what is important: "Talk about Jesus."

When the Lord Jesus gave instructions to His disciples before the Ascension, He said, *"Be my witnesses"* (Acts 1:8). That is, speak of Him--invite individuals to follow Him. When Philip witnessed to the Ethiopian eunuch, the Bible says simply, *"Philip told him the good news about Jesus"* (Acts 8:35). No more. No less.

It is especially important for cross-cultural workers, dealing with individuals from diverse cultures and varied religious systems, not to get hung up on anything that could keep individuals from seeing Christ alone. In many parts of the world, the word "Christian" no longer has such a precise meaning. The word "Christianity" has centuries of harmful baggage, and it often scares people away.

So our message is JESUS ONLY. When Christ is clearly and warmly presented, people in the most unlikely cultural/religious systems will quietly but dramatically become believers in Jesus.

What a privilege to present Him to potential followers all over the world. When He is lifted up, He will draw people to Himself.

> *"That is why God also raised Him up on high and gave Him the name above every other name that at the name of Jesus everyone in heaven and on earth and under the earth should kneel and everyone should confess, 'Jesus Christ is Lord!' and so glorify God the Father."*
>
> Philippians 2:9-11 (BECK)

52

WORLD TRAMPS

I really believe it's a privilege to be involved in our unique international ministry of cross-cultural interaction. How grateful we can be that, as Corrie ten Boom puts it, "We have been commissioned to be *world tramps* . . . who have left our hiding places to travel the gap with the Savior."

This is an amazing way of presenting the Good News about Jesus Christ to our generation. Both you and I have discovered that the true Church of Christ is multi-ethnic, worldwide, and universal.

It's too bad that we American missionaries too often delivered an "Americanized" version of the Gospel to various cultures and have inadvertently created "little Americas" rather than effectively reproducing Christian disciples. But we have learned through our mistakes. Today's missionary leaders are called to deliver *His Word* modeled by *Biblically authenticated lifestyles*.

In the process, we must avoid the temptation of seeking stardom. We cannot see ourselves as *chiefs* in ministry around the world. We cannot parade ourselves as "know-it-alls." There is no room for arrogance in ministry. Rather, as we minister, we must recognize our roles as *servants*.

We are called to be partners with Christ, and yet . . . partners also with other missionaries, national leaders, and with national believers. We are to be participants in a *cooperative endeavor*. To do this well, I'm discovering the value of learning from others.

The American way (even in ministry) is not the only way. Perhaps, it is not even the best way. There is much for us to learn.

Recently, I returned from 18 days of ministry in Brazil. Our first week was spent in a cooperative venture with the Southern Baptists in Rio. Over 200 Christians from America were involved in an intensive week of ministry. At the conclusion of the week, we had an open sharing session. One of my American brothers shared the following . . .

"I wish I could take some of these Brazilian Christians back home with me. These believers have a lot to teach us American Christians. We could learn from them . . . how to really be concerned for the lost . . . how to love each other with an "*abraco*" (that's Portuguese for "hug") . . . how to sing with enthusiasm . . . how to live simply . . . how to radiate the joy of the Lord on our faces . . . how to eagerly hunger for the Word. I have learned a lot from these brothers and sisters in Christ," he concluded.

There was spontaneous and sustained applause from the rest of us. We had gone to Brazil to bless and to minister; but in the process, *we were blessed* and ministered to by Brazilian believers.

It's interesting--I often find myself praying . . . "Lord, give me a heart to serve and bless others . . . a mind to stretch and grow . . . eyes and ears open to learn." If we could all pray this with intensity and sincerity, I believe that our effectiveness would grow. I want to learn . . . and grow . . . and be taught by Brazilian believers, Russian or Indian Christians . . . by "disciples from all nations." I have a lot to learn. Don't we all?

". . . it should be that of your inner self, the unfading beauty of a gentle and quiet spirit, which is of great worth in God's sight."
1 Peter 3:4 (NIV)

BACK TO BASICS

The cover and major story of a past issue of TIME magazine was entitled *"The Simple Life."* The descriptive subtitle was *"Rejecting the rat race, Americans get back to basics."* This seven-page article was most encouraging and quite incredible. In part it stated:

> "After a 10-year bender of gaudy dreams and godless consumerism, Americans are starting to trade down. They want to reduce their attachments to status symbols, fast-track careers and great expectations of Having It All. Upscale is out; downscale is in. Yuppies are an ancient civilization. Flaunting money is considered gauche: if you've got it, please keep it to yourself--or give some away.

> "In place of materialism, many Americans are embracing simpler pleasures and homier values. They've been thinking hard about what really matters in their lives, and they've decided to make some changes. What matters is having time for family and friends, rest and recreation, good deeds and spirituality. For some people that means a radical step: changing one's career, living on less, or packing up and moving to a quieter place. For others it can mean something as subtle as choosing a cheaper brand of running shoes or leaving work a little earlier to watch the kids in a soccer game.

> "The pursuit of a simpler life with deeper meaning is a major shift in America's private agenda."

Many of you have *already* embraced such a simple lifestyle. As I have visited some of you who serve as missionaries and Christian workers in remote parts of this world, I have usually been impressed with the absence of "things."

However, too many of us still have lives that are much too cluttered. I often think of the words of Jesus, *"Watch out! Be on your guard against all kinds of greed; a man's life does not consist in the abundance of his possessions"* (Luke 12:15, NIV).

Jesus told His followers, even as He sent them out into ministry, to travel lightly and simply. Indeed He not only instructed them to live and serve according to modest means, but He Himself modeled this ministry style as well. All of the elements surrounding His visit to earth illustrate this consistent principle of simplicity. Even at His birth, there was simplicity. The stable . . . His peasant mother . . . the simplicity of Bethlehem . . . the shepherds. God did not choose the finest accommodations nor the best known city in the area. He did not select a famous person to be the mother of Jesus nor did He choose the upper strata of society to be the first to welcome Jesus into the world. During Jesus' years of ministry He said that He did not even have a place on earth that He could call home. Jesus certainly never traveled "first class."

It was Abraham Lincoln who once said, "God must have loved the common man. He made so many of us."

Simplicity. Commonness. I like these words. I want them to characterize me. The servants of Christ have been called to embrace these qualities in our lives and ministries, just as they were modeled in the lives of Jesus and His Apostles.

Just this morning, Evie and I had breakfast with a longtime friend. Years ago when we first met, he was a well-paid lawyer in a prestigious legal firm with an abundance of worldly possessions. He had the "good life" with a secure future. Yet, he sensed a call

56

of God to leave all of these things and to follow Jesus Christ into a ministry position that necessitated a major adjustment in lifestyle. He now directs a significant ministry that is making a profound impact for God.

For all of us, a move toward the simple lifestyle could be the best move we ever made. Or at least to a *simpler* lifestyle.

> Friends all around us are trying to find
> What the heart yearns for, by sin undermined;
> I know the secret, I know where 'tis found,
> Only in Jesus true pleasures abound.
>
> All that I want is in Jesus;
> He satisfies, with joy He supplies;
> Life would be worthless without Him,
> All things in Jesus I find.
>
> --Harry Dixon Loes

BLURRED VISION

The memory is still vivid. I was a sophomore in high school. I had been having some trouble with my vision. I went to the optometrist for a thorough eye examination. The doctor diagnosed three problems: (1) eyestrain, (2) astigmatism, and (3) over-convergence of the lens. The doctor explained that astigmatism simply meant "indistinctness of vision" and that overconvergence meant that my eyes crossed at close-ranged objects.

And so I received my first pair of glasses to improve my vision. I will never forget the first time I looked at the outdoors with my new glasses. *Wow, were things ever clear, sharp, and bright!* I couldn't believe how my vision had deteriorated and how much better I could see with the new glasses.

Through the years, of course, I've made many return visits to the optometrist's office for an eye examination and, always, an adjustment to improve my vision. In fact, just yesterday I again was examined and refitted for better and clearer vision.

As a pilgrim and servant in Christ's ministry, it has often been necessary for me to be alone with the GREAT OPTOMETRIST for a personal examination of my *spiritual* vision. Frequently, I have needed correction for my "indistinctness of vision." There are probably a lot of reasons that our spiritual vision becomes blurred. Distractions are too tempting . . . too numerous . . . too persuasive.

What really is most important in life and ministry? What should our primary focus be?

If you ask the man on the street, "What is the greatest theme in the world?" you might get these answers: *Success. Prestige. Fame. Pleasure. Money. Security. Happiness.* Sadly, all of these are inadequate answers.

If you ask the man in the pew, you might get an entirely different list: *Evangelism. Missions. Love. Spiritual Gifts. Discipleship. Eternity. Salvation. Prayer. Commitment. Ministry.* These, too, are great themes and perhaps even more worthy goals. However, even these aren't the primary reasons for which we are to live and serve.

What then is to be our spiritual focus? Upon what do we base our life and ministry? There is only one answer . . . *the Glory of God.*

That idea is amplified in the traditional Westminster Catechism:

> *"Man's chief aim is to glorify God and to enjoy Him forever."*

H.C. Thiessen, in his classic book, *Systematic Theology*, says:

> "The end of all things is the glory of God and only as we also adopt this as our real goal in life are we living on the highest plane and in full harmony with the purposes of God."

Is it time for a visit to the DIVINE OPTOMETRIST? Maybe you were fitted some time ago for clearer vision, but is it time for another examination?

> "Fill all my vision, Savior, I pray. Let me see only Jesus today. Though through the valley, Thou leadest me. Give me Thy glory and beauty to see."
> --Avis B. Christiansen

THE VALUE OF FORGIVENESS

It's a grim thought, but sometimes it's healthy (and no doubt even *necessary*) to be gripped with the awfulness of *our own sinfulness.* Only then are we able to be appropriately grateful to the Lord for His incredible gift of FORGIVENESS.

I wonder if we give enough thought to just how great a Biblical theme forgiveness is. It might be *the most welcomed gift* that we received when we first trusted Christ. It continues to be good news as we from time to time reckon with the awfulness of our past sins and the continuous reality of new temptations and sins trying to crowd into our lives.

Imagine the relief sensed by the woman caught in the act of adultery when Jesus spoke these words: *"Your sins are forgiven."*

And think of the powerful impact on the crowd gathered at Pentecost when Peter said, "Repent for the forgiveness of sins." The message of FORGIVENESS was also preeminent in the preaching of the early pastors as indicated with Paul's message at Pisidian, Antioch, when he proclaimed, *"I preach the forgiveness of sins through Jesus to you."* When Paul catalogs the benefits enjoyed by believers in his letters to the Ephesian church and the Colossian church, he mentions *"the forgiveness of sins."*

And in the Old Testament, David often spoke personally about the forgiveness of sin. He certainly knew much about personal failure . . . gross sin . . . and the negative consequences of unconfessed sin. David had a crucial first-hand experience with debilitating guilt. Often he cried out to God. Psalm 130 is especially helpful:

> Twice David cries out to the Lord for relief. (vs. 1-2)
> He spoke of the "depths" of despair. (vs. 1)
> He recognized his need for the Lord's "mercy." (vs. 2)

And then David speaks these amazing words to the Lord (vs.3-4):

> *"If you, O Lord, kept a record of sins, O Lord, who could stand? But with you there is forgiveness."*

David had a clear sense of his sinfulness. And this also gave him an understanding of his unworthiness before God. But David also affirmed the truth that God, in grace and mercy, offers total, unreserved forgiveness to His children.

Did you catch the depth of David's question? He asked, "O Lord, if you kept a record of sins, who could stand?" Good question! And the answer . . . *nobody!* David couldn't stand. I couldn't. You couldn't. *None of us would have a ghost of a chance* of standing before a righteous God. We would all be without hope.

But, God does *not* keep a record of our sins. That's right. Believers are forgiven. *Absolutely.* And when He forgives us, He actually forgets our sins . . . blots them out . . . *forever!*

We need to celebrate forgiveness with holy exhilaration. It's even permissible to shout with a resounding, "*I am forgiven!*"

Maybe you needed this thought right now. Have past sins come back to haunt and intimidate you? Is your thought life a bit undisciplined? Is the tongue acting up? God's good news . . . as you confess, HE FORGIVES and CLEANSES. *He really does!*

> *"If we confess our sins, He is faithful and just and will forgive our sins and purify us from all unrighteousness."*
>
> 1 John 1:9 (NIV)

61

DON'T BE A NOODNIK

Have you ever heard of a *noodnik*? I learned this term, along with millions of others, from columnist Ann Landers. She says it's a yiddish term meaning "one who spreads cheer by *not* showing up." That's right . . . by *not* showing up. His absence is better than his presence.

I hope that never describes *me!* Or, if it ever did, that it never again will typify me. The Christian, in total contrast to the noodnik, is to spread cheer . . . and joy . . . and blessing . . . *by his presence.* We are to be encouragers.

Whatever else God wants me to do and be, I know that He wants me to be an encourager. Chuck Swindoll writes, "I know of no one more needed, more valuable, more Christ-like, than the person who is committed to encouragement."

So you are a doctor . . . a teacher . . . a Bible translator . . . a student . . . an administrator. Fine. But are you an encouraging doctor . . . an encouraging teacher . . . an encouraging Bible translator . . . an encouraging student . . . an encouraging administrator?

Does your life bring cheer along your pathway? Are your words sensitive and uplifting? In the home and on the job, does your presence bring a ray of hope? Are you nudging people toward a closer walk with the Lord with the quality of your inner joy, character, and encouragement?

All around us are desperate people. Weary. Discouraged. Misunderstood. Ready to "throw in the towel." If they haven't given up completely, they've likely resigned themselves to a life of miserable, intolerable, debilitating mediocrity.

How different their daily existence might be if you would touch them with *encouragement* . . . by some positive, uplifting word, a caring smile, a friendly hug, a nugget of eternal truth. *You* could be used of God to make the difference.

The Lord has given me a unique ministry and unusual challenge. One of the ways we try to help encourage others is through our monthly devotional letter. God willing, when I come into your life for a moment each month, talking to you from my desk to yours, I want to do two things. First, I want to encourage you . . . to love and lift you . . . to believe not just in you but also in the incredible impact that you already have for God or the remarkable effect you *might* have as He works through you.

Secondly, I want to urge you to be an encourager. You might say, "Well, at least I'm not a *noodnik*--people aren't cheered by my absence." Nevertheless, we can do better at encouraging others.

I agree with William Barclay when he says, "One of the highest of human duties is the duty of encouragement. It is easy to laugh at men's ideals; it is easy to pour cold water on their enthusiasm; it is easy to discourage others. The world is full of discouragers. We have a duty to encourage one another. Many a time a word of praise, or thanks, or appreciation, or cheer has kept a man on his feet. Blessed is the one who speaks such a word."

Often the Apostle Paul wrote letters, and his words were always reassuring and encouraging. Yet he was always hoping for the greater reality of face-to-face meeting with friends. Of course, personal meetings are better, but when that's impossible--the letter is truly a blessing.

> *"A cheerful heart is good medicine, but a*
> *crushed spirit dries up the bones."*
> Proverbs 17:22 (NIV)

RISKY BUSINESS

It is risky business to be involved in Christian ministry, especially service in worldwide missions. Perhaps you've never really thought about it, but there are a lot of risks to deal with along the way. It's certainly wise to "count the cost" as Jesus instructed, as you proceed with single-minded determination to serve Him.

If you're involved in ministry, think back to your initial call from the Lord. Recall the thoughts that first ran through your mind, and later dominated your mind. Perhaps you asked:

> -- but what if I say "yes" to God and then can't raise my support; or
> -- what if I get some strange disease overseas; or
> -- what if my going is misunderstood or criticized by my family; or
> -- what if my spouse or loved one doesn't want to go; or
> -- what if I face persecution or worse; or
> -- what if I am killed in the line of duty for Christ?

If you're involved in Christian ministry, you once considered the *possibility* of these risks. Now you are experiencing the *reality* of these risks. Yes, indeed, there are risks. Not just those listed above, but others as well. We could fill pages of a book with such a listing of the risks of serving Christ.

Some months ago, Evie and I were on a Wycliffe assignment in Colombia, South America. Just a few years ago, one of their young translators, Chester Bitterman, was captured by the M-19 terrorist organization. He was, after about a month of terrible abuse, finally murdered. I motorcycled to the little cemetery at Loma Linda and visited his gravesite. I knelt by the tombstone and recommitted myself to Christ and His worldwide ministry. I had always had a full recognition of the possible risks, yet as I prayed beside Chet Bitterman's grave, I was more acutely aware of them. Still, I promised God that I'd continue to follow and serve Him.

Paul and Barnabas, two exemplary first-century servants, are described in Acts 15:26 as two men "who have *risked* their lives for the name of our Lord Jesus Christ." That word *"risked"* is translated variously by other translators. . . . Weymouth says *"endangered"*; Berkeley says *"jeopardized"*; and the TCNT says *"sacrificed."* All of these help us understand that Paul and Barnabas were totally committed to Christ and the task of worldwide missions *despite the dangerous risks involved*.

Here is the good news. I assure you, based on the authority of the Scriptures, of two truths pertaining to the risk:

> *First, the cause of Jesus Christ is worth the risk.*
> *Second, the ultimate reward for servants is worth the risk.*

Never . . . never . . . never, in the rough and tumble of life, forget these two great truths.

Let's link arms together with the valiant, gutsy men and women who have journeyed before us with unswerving allegiance to Jesus.

> "The entrance fee into the Kingdom of Heaven is nothing. But the annual subscription is everything."
> --Henry Drummond

> *"Jesus said . . . 'If anyone would come after me, he must deny himself and take up his cross and follow me. For whoever wants to save his life will lose it, but whoever loses his life for me will find it.' "*
> Matthew 16:24-25 (NIV)

THE FAITH FACTOR

Today I need to think about "trusting God." I hope that doesn't sound too glib or trite, but listen in. Maybe you--like me--find yourself saying with the disciples, "Lord, increase my faith."

There are at least two types of faith. There is SAVING FAITH, which is initial faith by which we came to Christ. Then, there is LIVING FAITH, which is subsequent faith. This second phase of faith is lauded in the Scriptures as a prime factor in the maturing of God's people.

Four times, spanning both the Old and the New Testaments, the FAITH PRINCIPLE is stated in these simple words, "The just shall live by faith." The writer of Hebrews adds to the importance of the PRINCIPLE by stating that . . . "without faith, it is impossible to please God."

Admittedly, it is often difficult to trust God with our lives. And yet, I find it easy to trust the local banker with my money . . . the pilot (whom I do not even know) with getting me to my travel destination . . . and the cook (whom I have also never met) with my nourishment. It doesn't make sense, does it?

God is faithful, worthy of our trust. All of the biblical authors speak of His faithfulness as an intrinsic attribute of His divine nature. He is totally trustworthy, thoroughly dependable, and utterly faithful. It's because He is faithful that He can be trusted without question.

Some time ago, a Bible translator of an Indian language group in Guatemala shared this insight with me. He was wanting to accurately translate "trust." As he struggled with this word, an Indian mother carrying her infant son on her back, wrapped in the traditional shawl, walked by his window. The infant son was resting comfortably and securely on his mother's back. The son knew no fear, no anxiety, and no concern. Instantly the translator had a word picture of the meaning of "trust." Used in our relationship to God, it is this: "trusting God is resting our heart upon the strong and sturdy back of our heavenly Father."

But how does this affect you and me? Especially when we are unappreciated by those we are serving? When pain comes to us through a rebellious child? When physical health begins to unravel? When financial support is slow and insufficient? When "the work" is all-consuming? When you feel ready to "throw in the towel" and go home? How does all of this affect the FAITH PRINCIPLE?

Faith has no power in itself--God provides the power. Faith, then, is that attitude of soul that enables us to find and use that power. When life is difficult, it is then that our faith has an unprecedented opportunity for growth.

Job, after the process whereby he lost everything, declared, "Though He slay me, yet will I trust Him (God)." In fact, Job's difficulties cemented his relationship to God. Job is our model that life consists of both mountain and valley experiences.

> "Through it all, through it all . . .
> I've learned to trust in Jesus, I've learned to trust in God.

> "Through it all, through it all . . .
> I've learned to depend on His Word."

--Andre Crouch

(C) Manna Music Co.
Used by Permission

WHO, ME? -- WITNESS?

I was challenged by an incident one of our Board members once shared with me. A troubled employee came into his office "just to talk." In the course of the quiet conversation, the president was able to share the Gospel of Jesus Christ with his employee who then prayed to become a follower of the Lord.

I had known this Board member for over twenty years. He looked for witnessing opportunities, taking advantage of them when God opened doors. Sharing Christ was a natural part of his lifestyle.

I was preaching at a conference for missionaries in Africa some time ago. Following one of the services, a physician came to me and said, "Thank you for nudging us into sharing our faith with people. I have become so involved in dealing with the physical ills of my patients that I have neglected telling them of Christ."

Jesus told *all of His followers* to . . . "Be my witnesses." Many of us rationalize this command or talk ourselves out of *personal* responsibility. Perhaps we contribute money so that professional evangelists can witness on our behalf. Or, maybe we practice a "silent witness." We ask, "Isn't it more important just to live the life and let them see Jesus in me?"

The answer is Yes and No. Yes . . . it's important to live a consistent life. But, no, it's not enough to live a good life, for several reasons. First, none of us lives *that good a life* that our excellence alone will bring people to Christ. Second, even if our life is exceptional but we never share our faith verbally, it is conceivable that in their last moments of life, our friends and loved ones could think back and question, "I wonder what it was about Bill that made him so radiant and alive?"

The Gospel needs to be verbalized.

James Kennedy in his book, *Evangelism Explosion*, states that 95% of all Christians have never led another person to Christ. *What a dramatic indictment of believers!* But I believe that can change. If you and I pray daily for witness opportunities, and then if we take advantage of these opportunities that God brings into our lives, Christians can have a worldwide impact.

It doesn't matter who you are or where you live. Or what you do. Jesus addressed *all* of His followers when He told them to be His witnesses. If you live in the States, be His witness. If you are located overseas, whether in administration, translation, music ministry . . . or working with cars, computers, or any other vocation, pray for opportunities to share Christ. Then, in His power and by His Spirit, take advantage of the doors that He opens.

My thanks go to the late Erv Parr, the Christian businessman and Barnabas board member, who was my role model for a lifestyle evangelist. Thanks, too, belong to Erv for nudging you and me to do *more* in this direction. No one better exemplified the model given by the Apostle Peter who admonished us to "be ready always to give an answer to any man. . . ."

> "Give me a passion for souls, dear Lord . . .
> A passion to save the lost.
> O that Thy love were by all adored,
> And welcomed at any cost.
>
> "Jesus, I long, I long to be winning
> Men who are lost, and constantly sinning. . .
> O may this hour be one of beginning
> The story of pardon to tell."
>
> --Herbert Tovey

HIDING BEHIND MASKS

In the spring of 1989, my son and I spent a few hours in Venice, Italy, between ministry stops in Salzburg and Vienna. It was beautiful and yet *bizarre*.

I had always heard about the captivating charm of Venice . . . surrounded by water and frequently intersected with canals . . . beautiful, stunning, and unique. But I was not prepared for the other distinction of the city . . . the *masks*.

We made a visit to the town square and visited many of the shops in the streets surrounding the square. Everywhere, masks were for sale . . . sold by street vendors . . . displayed in the stores and in some specialty shops that sold *only* masks.

There were all kinds of masks . . . masks to hang on the wall, to set on a shelf, and especially to wear on your face. The masks were made of just about every conceivable construction--cardboard, papier-mache, metal, feathers, and ceramics. All were priced moderately to very expensive.

And people were wearing masks. I'm not sure if it was for some holiday or carnival, but everywhere we looked, everyone was wearing masks--adults as well as kids. The masks kept all of us guessing as to who was behind them. Some people owned many different masks . . . with a face for all occasions. Yes, it was strange . . . bizarre is the right word to describe it.

After the brief visit, we were back on the train. But my mind could not forget the scene. As I pondered it all, I thought of the teaching of Jesus. Seven times (Matthew 23), He chided the super-religious Pharisees for being hypocrites . . . pretenders, actors, MASK-WEARERS. He explains the essence of hypocrisy by saying:

"You clean the outside of the cup and dish, but inside they are full of greed and self-indulgence. First clean the inside of the cup and dish, and then the outside also will be clean. . . . In the same way, on the outside you appear to people as righteous but on the inside you are full of hypocrisy and wickedness" (Matthew 23:25, 26, 28, NIV).

Jesus also spoke to *His disciples* about the potential danger of hypocrisy. Four times in the Sermon on the Mount He uses the word again . . . hypocrisy in our service, hypocrisy in our prayer lives, hypocrisy in our fasting, and hypocrisy in our harsh judgment of one another. He tells us to *"take the plank out of your own eyes, and then you will see clearly to remove the specks from your brother's eyes"* (Matthew 7:5, NIV).

Peter, in his first Epistle, also tells us believers to rid ourselves of our *hypocrisies*. Do we believers need such advice? Unfortunately *we do*. Even in our innermost being, in the core of our ministry, in our motivation for ministry, and in our impartial treatment of each other, we need the warning. Hypocrisy is an ever present threat.

There is always the need for a clear call to genuineness, authenticity, and sincerity. A call to TAKE OFF THE MASK. And when the mask is off, might there be a very real, godly person in the process of being re-created into the very image of the Lord Jesus.

"Therefore, rid yourselves of all malice and all deceit, hypocrisy, envy and slander of every kind."
1 Peter 2:1 (TLB)

DO-IT-YOURSELF ENCOURAGEMENT

Barnabas International was started as a means of bringing encouragement to Christ's servants around the world. A case in point was a trip I took to the Ivory Coast of Africa where I spent two weeks in ministry to missionaries from several mission boards. I preached much of the time, but also spent many hours in formal and informal conversations with individual missionaries.

During these "one on one" exchanges, many expressed a variety of feelings: loneliness, frustration, self-doubt, pressure, and fatigue. One said, "Do I really have what it takes to be a missionary?"

Another told me of feeling stretched, pulled in too many directions.

Many of these Christian servants needed to be encouraged. *But, don't we all?* A common thread that unites all humanity, including those of us in ministry, is that *we need to be encouraged.* Often that encouragement comes from the Christian community (that is, the group of people with whom we live, work, and serve). Sometimes that encouragement comes from an individual. I often pray that our "Fraternity" (and "Sorority") of Barnabas will spread greatly throughout the world in bringing love, support, and encouragement to the people of God.

But at times, the Christian community lets us down. Sometimes there is no encourager around when we need one the most. *Then what do we do?*

When David was hated and hunted by Saul . . . when the Philistines were a constant threat to him and his people . . . when he was separated from his family and others that he loved . . . when the enemy threatened to stone him . . . when he wept until he had no more strength left to weep, what did he do?

The Scriptures tell us that **David encouraged *himself* in the Lord** (1 Samuel 30:6). And the Psalms are an inspiring record of his search for this encouragement. Sometimes that is exactly what *we* have to do. We must build our relationship with the Lord and find Him to be our Sufficiency . . . our Joy . . . our Refuge.

In the good times of life, we need to build up our spiritual and emotional resource to prepare for darker days. We have learned from experience that the dark days *do* come. And when the distressing times come upon us, we must learn to lean on Him. Ultimately, He is the Healer, the Encourager, the Helper.

But what does all this mean? Here are some suggestions:

1. Learn to *spend time daily with Him.*

2. Take *spiritual breaks*. Throughout the day these can be times of renewal. (David's harp got a lot of use!)

3. *Practice praise*, even when you don't feel like it just as David did.

4. Occasionally take a day, or even a half-day, for a *personal spiritual retreat*, all alone with Him and the Book, talking with Him and having Him talk with you.

5. *Reach out to others*. Often there's healing and personal encouragement as you reach out in ministry.

As I pray for you, I hope you'll pray for me, and together we'll discover the great resource of ENCOURAGING OURSELVES.

> *"When I cried Thou answeredst me, and strengthenest me with strength in my soul."*
> Psalm 138:3 (KJV)

PAYING THE PRICE

"Suffer hardship with me, as a good soldier of Christ Jesus. No soldier in active service entangles himself in the affairs of everyday life, so that he may please the one who enlisted him as a soldier. And also if anyone competes as an athlete, he does not win the prize unless he competes according to the rules. The hard-working farmer ought to be the first to receive his share of the crops."

2 Timothy 2:3-6 (NIV)

Paul's exhortation to his young colleague in ministry is appropriate for all of us to hear and to heed. He uses three illustrations . . .

- the hard-working **farmer.**
- the self-disciplined **soldier.**
- the totally committed **athlete.**

In each situation, the person Paul describes is singularly committed to the task and has his eye fixed *not just on the goal* but on the ultimate reward.

That person chooses to have the long look instead of the short focus--sees value in the distance race versus the quick short dash.

Dallas Green, manager of the New York Yankees, had this motto on the wall of the clubhouse at the winter training center in Fort Lauderdale, Florida:

"THE WILL TO WIN IS NOT WORTH A NICKEL
UNLESS YOU HAVE THE WILL TO PRACTICE."

Undoubtedly, all of us want to be winners in the Christian life . . . as well as in our respective fields of Christian service.

BUT THE PRICE TAG . . . yes, the *price tag* for winning . . . is total commitment . . . hard work . . . self-discipline.

I think that it's true, not only for the baseball player . . . farmer . . . soldier . . . or athlete. It's true for *every* discipline of life. Think about it. The accomplished pianist knows the rigors of long hours of tedious practice. The college professor also knows the discipline of study and the singular focus of hard work.

All of this truth is transferable to Christian living and service. The Christian faith is an active lifestyle based on commitment and discipline. If anything in life is worth 100%, our calling in Christ must head the list. And if anyone is worthy of this loyalty, Jesus is.

I genuinely want to finish my life and ministry hearing the words of Jesus, *"Well done, thou good and faithful servant!"*

But that will only happen if today I am completely focused on Him every day. . . rehearsing for Ultimate Glory . . . working hard.

Without today's effort, great goals are merely empty drama . . . unrealistic expectations . . . vague aspirations.

> *"So then, just as you have received Christ Jesus as Lord, continue to live in him, rooted and built up in him, strengthened in the faith as you were taught, and overflowing with thankfulness."*
> Colossians 2:6-7 (NIV)

WRESTLING IN PRAYER

All of us know the value of prayer support. There have been some special times . . . when the load is unusually heavy, when the schedule is incredibly tight, when the body is tired and our emotions stretched thin . . . that we have sensed God's strength and we suddenly became buoyant as our spirits soared. Often at that moment, I *know* that someone is praying.

The intercessory prayers of God's people can make an effective difference. We've seen it happen too often to deny its reality. Yet, while we bathe in the blessings of the prayers of others *for us*, we're reminded to also participate in intercessory prayers *for others*. The apostle Paul stressed both sides of this coin frequently.

I have found the Epistle to the Colossians especially helpful in giving me guidance about intercessory prayer. This epistle tells us *how to intercede for others*.

We are to **intercede thankfully**. *"We always thank God . . . when we pray for you"* (Colossians 1:3, NIV). When we bring the names of others to His throne, it is not to be with a sigh, nor a groan, but with thanksgiving.

We are to **intercede continuously**. *"We have not stopped praying for you"* (Colossians 1:9a, NIV). Our prayer lists should be used not just in our quiet times but throughout the day as God brings the names of individuals to us. Day and night, we can be intercessors.

We are to **intercede meaningfully**. Paul's prayers were weighty-- meaty, filled with content and substance. Such as this typical one:
"We are asking God to fill you with the knowledge of his will through all spiritual wisdom and understanding. And we pray this in order that you may live a life worthy of the Lord and may please him in every way; bearing fruit in

76

every good work, growing in the knowledge of God, being strengthened with all power according to his glorious might so that you have great endurance and patience, and joyfully giving thanks to the Father who has qualified you to share in the inheritance of the saints in the kingdom of light." Colossians 1:9-12 (NIV)

Pray this prayer if you don't know what to pray for your loved ones. I'd love to know others were praying this powerful prayer for me.

We are to *intercede specifically*. Paul asked for others to pray specifically for him and gave them three specific requests to remember (Colossians 4:2-4). Pray with *specificity* . . . for specific people and for specific requests. I recently saw a cartoon of a man kneeling by his bed for his nightly prayer: *"So I beseech your mercy, et cetera, et cetera, usual closing, JBW."* Unfortunately, it's too accurate to dismiss as a simple cartoon. Let *us* so intercede.

We are to *intercede fervently*. Paul commended his friend, Epaphras, for being fervent in his prayer life as he wrote: *"Epaphras . . . is always wrestling in prayer for you"* (Colossians 4:12). Imagine! *Wrestling in prayer*, from the Greek root *agon* meaning agony, struggle, fight, war. Intercessory prayer is hard.

Wesley Duewel in his excellent book, *Touch the World Through Prayer*, gives the picture of the intercessor as One who stands in the gap--with one hand in God's hand, the other in the hand of the one for whom he prays. What a powerful potential for us as meaningful intercessors.

> *"Confess your faults to one another, and pray for one another . . . the effectual fervent prayer of a righteous man availeth much."*
> James 5:16 (KJV)

TWIN PROMISES

My first childhood recollection is a mission story. I was about five years old when it happened. After a Sunday service at my church in Minneapolis, most of our congregation went to the train station to see Liz Anderson off for a five-year term in Africa. I can't forget my feelings and tears as a child. Five years was too long and Africa was so far. But I didn't know then what I know now.

When Jesus gave the Great Commission to His disciples (Matthew 28:18-20), He also gave them two great promises. Without them, the assignment would have been overwhelming, frightening, even impossible. But His two promises made all the difference not only for His disciples but for we who are twentieth-century disciples.

THE PROMISE OF HIS PRESENCE

Jesus promised to be with His followers *forever* . . . in all places and for all time (vs. 20). Previously God had promised the same to Joshua with these words, *"As I was with Moses, so I will be with you. I will never leave you nor forsake you."* In the Book of Psalms, He made the same promise to David.

The promise of His abiding presence is also passed to God's people from generation to generation. Recently, Evie and I visited missionaries in the jungle areas of the Ivory Coast of Africa. A few days later we left for Europe and ministered in some of the large cities there. God's presence was with us as we flew to Africa . . . stayed with us in its dark jungles . . . and continued with us as we traveled to the bustling cities of Europe. The promise of God's presence is also for you who are in the crowded cities of the world and to those in the isolated villages as well.

You and I are never alone. Sometimes *lonely* . . . but ***never alone!***

THE PROMISE OF HIS POWER

Jesus assured His disciples that all authority and power was His to give to them. He gives us, two thousand years later, that same authority to empower our lives and ministries (vs. 18).

All of us in ministry go through times of powerlessness. This helplessness often leads to hopelessness, then discouragement. Such times surface in many different ways. Even now, perhaps you are facing such a time and circumstances. Maybe you are tired (physically and/or emotionally). Or you might be spiritually weary, wondering if your efforts are making a difference and frustrated with the enormity of your assignment. Has the chill of loneliness and separation numbed you? Do you feel misunderstood? Ready to throw in the towel? *Then this promise is for you.*

Jesus promises His power. Power to revitalize you. Power to refresh you. Power to bless you and to bless others through you. Power to make your talents and gifts effective as they are coupled with His great authority.

When Peter discovered God's power for his life and ministry, he moved from weakness to strength. From his personal experience, Peter confidently wrote these words for our encouragement:

> *"His divine power has given us everything we need for life and godliness."*
>
> 2 Peter 1:3 (NIV)

I'd never dare step out in ministry unless I was assured of these two promised realities: ***His Presence and Power go with me!***

> *"I will not leave you comfortless: I will come to you."*
>
> 1 John 14:18 (NIV)

SEEK TO SERVE

When I graduated from Minnehaha Academy, our class motto was "To serve, and not to be served." In retrospect, our high school class chose a great motto . . . a biblical concept . . . a most worthy phrase to steer us into lives of usefulness to Christ and humanity. I don't know why the concept of serving others is so misunderstood and neglected.

Jesus valued servanthood in His followers. In fact, He stated some radical ideas about it:

> *"Whoever wants to be great among you must be your servant . . . and whoever wants to be first must be your slave."*   Matthew 20:27 (NIV)

He also said:

> *"The Son of Man did not come to be served but to serve, and to give His life a ransom for many."*
>   Matthew 20:28 (NIV)

Jesus stated the principle not only to help steer His followers, but in so doing He demonstrated servanthood in His own life and ministry. Paul says that it was Christ's mindset of servanthood that brought Him from heaven to earth (Philippians 2:5-8). His lifestyle of servanthood was clearly displayed in His three-year ministry. When Jesus washed His disciples' feet, He humbly yet dramatically showed them that servanthood involves stooping and ministering to lowly but necessary needs of others (John 13).

It's an interesting concept that is fully at odds with today's philosophy of self-gratification and personal satisfaction. But *we are called to be servants* . . . servants of the Lord and to each other.

80

It is impossible to separate the two sides of the coin of servanthood:

> **SERVANTS OF THE LORD**. The early apostles cherished this title and often began their epistles with this phrase affirming their relationship to the Lord.

> **SERVANTS TO EACH OTHER**. Repeatedly, we are called *to serve one another*. It is especially imperative that all of us in the Christian ministry embrace servanthood as a primary characteristic of our lives--serving each other, not lording it over each other--serving, not dominating. But we'll have to admit that many of us have much to learn about Christian servanthood.

God's will for us involves our developing the servant's heart . . . having the servant's mindset . . . and fulfilling the servant's lifestyle. We see in the Scriptures and affirm it by our own experience--servanthood is not taught in the world at large, so cannot be easily learned. We learn it at Jesus' feet.

Hear it clearly. We are NOT called to live like kings, but as servants. We are NOT to pursue status, but service. We are NOT to be Christian celebrities. There are too many of these strutting around already. We are called to be Christian servants--and there are two few of these walking around today. After all, this period of history is more than ever the day for service.

Several years ago after speaking in chapel at Taylor University, I received a gift from Jay Kesler and Bob Griffin, then the President and Chaplain of this great Christian school.

The gift? It was a servant's towel. The towel had the logo of Taylor University, the printed text of John 13, and these words, *"Jesus, our Example of Servanthood,"* written on it.

I was told that every graduate of Taylor University receives two things at commencement . . . a diploma . . . and A SERVANT'S TOWEL. I thought, how very significant.

Without the servant's towel, you and I are not ready for effective ministry. And to borrow the phrase of that popular TV commercial, "Never leave home without it!"

> *"Humble yourselves, therefore, under God's mighty hand, that He may lift you up in due time."*
>
> 1 Peter 5:6 (NIV)

A KING WITHOUT A THRONE

Recently, my wife, Evie, and I, with a small group of friends, had a serendipity experience . . . a warm, unexpected surprise. We had just finished a conference in Frankfurt, West Germany and went to spend several days with friends near Bavaria. One afternoon we made a half-day visit to Neuschwanstein, one of the castles of King Ludwig II. Perhaps you have seen a picture of this famous castle, sitting high in the Alps. The castle is large, elaborate, and imposing. But it has been uninhabited for the last hundred years.

Our guide showed us through numerous hallways and exquisitely decorated rooms. We were struck by its assault on our senses. *Amazing. Lavish. Unbelievable.* The most memorable room to me was the throne room. Inside were breathtaking wonders--two thousand-pound chandeliers, mosaic floor, and other extravagant fixtures.

But there was no throne in the throne room . . . because the king had run out of money! How ironic. Imagine a king . . . WITHOUT A THRONE.

But while that was memorable, that was not the most impressive thing about the throne room to me. Our guide pointed out a painting of Christ on the ceiling, above where the throne was to have been situated, and then he said to us,

> "You will notice that in this throne room there is the
> painting of Jesus Christ, the King of kings and Lord
> of lords."

That's all the guide said, but it was enough to bring a stir to my soul, a tear to my eye, and an inner assurance that Jesus is indeed *King of kings and Lord of lords*.

Even while visiting this impressive and majestic residence of a human king, we were reminded that there is an *even greater King*.

Human history, past and present, is filled with the memorable names of prominent individuals . . . kings, prime ministers, presidents, authors, entertainers . . . those who enter the "stage" of life, stay briefly, and are quickly forgotten.

Even today there are prominent names in the newspapers . . . Clinton, Major, Yeltsin, Arafat. Yesterday, the names in the news were Reagan, Bush, Thatcher, Gorbechev. They appeared briefly on the world's stage, made a contribution, and left. Sometimes we wonder, who is really in control? Who will be the ultimate winner? Where is history headed?

It is true that the human players change from time to time. But only ONE has been destined to be KING forever. The ultimate WINNER. The LORD of history. John predicts the day when Christ shall return and "He has this name written . . . KING OF KINGS AND LORD OF LORDS" (Revelation 19:16).

Sometimes our assignments are difficult.

The opposition is stiff. Our enemies . . . and *the Enemy* . . . are oppressive. The results of our labor are slow and discouraging. Sometimes it even looks like the forces of evil are winning. But hear it again, this time from the pen of the Apostle Paul:

> *"Therefore, God exalted him to the highest place and gave him a Name that is above every name, that at the name of Jesus every knee should bow, in heaven and on earth and under the earth, and every tongue confess that Jesus Christ is Lord, to the glory of God the Father."*
>
> Philippians 2:9-11 (NIV)

REALITIES OF SPIRITUAL WARFARE

We were halfway through a seven-week pastoral residence at the jungle headquarters of the Peruvian Wycliffe ministry where I had been studying and preaching from Ephesians 6:10-20, the paragraph of Spiritual Warfare. Earlier that summer God convinced me to preach this series even before I realized the need for such a study.

We have learned that where there are mighty works for God being done, there is an inverse proportion of spiritual warfare. Christian workers are under attack everywhere. But I became increasingly aware of it in many parts of the world as we visited these centers of great spiritual struggles on behalf of Barnabas International.

I'm not sure that all Christians realize that there is a need for all of us to be taught the realities of Spiritual Warfare. What are some of these realities?

REALITY ONE:
>There is a spiritual fight, a struggle going on in the world. There always has been a raging war but perhaps only now are we becoming more aware of it.

REALITY TWO:
>Satan is the brilliant and strong leader of this rebellion against believers.

REALITY THREE:
>Satan is assisted by a vast, unbelievable army of evil spirits.

REALITY FOUR:
>Our struggle is not always against physical and visible people but against these agents of evil--as well as Satan,

himself--who are the **real and unseen enemies behind the evil that we do see.**

REALITY FIVE:

It is possible for us to be strong and victorious through the power of God. *"Be strong in the Lord and in his mighty power"* (Ephesians 6:10).

Yes, Satan is also strong . . . BUT HE IS NOT INVINCIBLE, NOR IS HE OMNIPOTENT. Remember that! Only God is omnipotent. All power is under His sovereign control. The Lord God offers to live in us and through us, making us strong in the battle. Remember, too, this companion text: *"Greater is He that is in you than he that is in the world"* (1 John 4:4, NASB).

REALITY SIX:

God has given us His suit of armor to wear. This is not just a reassuring metaphor. It gives us the protection that we need against Satan. The Armor of God has six pieces.

Four of these are to be worn on the body: the Belt of Truth, the Breastplate of Righteousness, the Shoes of Peace, and the Helmet of Salvation. The fifth piece is the Shield of Faith, which we are to alertly and aggressively carry before us. The sixth piece is the Sword of the Word which we are again to use militantly. Each piece of armor is to be literally put in place daily.

Prayerfully, we are to clothe ourselves for life, for ministry, and for battle. This is to be a decisive and deliberate action. We will not otherwise be victorious apart from wearing God's armor.

Nor are we to be simply passively involved. Twice in this text we are told to "put it on." Yes, there is something for us to do.

REALITY SEVEN:

Intercessory prayer is an important discipline to be exercised within the Christian community. We need a network of prayer for one another. We can cross distant miles through prayer . . . we can penetrate places otherwise inaccessible . . . we can stand with each other through prayer. Prayer is a formidable weapon as well.

REALITY EIGHT:

It is possible both to STAND . . . and to KEEP STANDING. The word *stand* is found four times in this paragraph of Scripture. Though the battle rages around us . . . though our troubles pile up within us . . . though Satan hurls his darts at us . . . God's promise is that *we can keep on standing . . . Christ is our victory!*

"What, then, shall we say in response to this? If God is for us, who can be against us?"

"No, in all these things we are more than conquerors through Him who loved us."
Romans 8:31b, 37 (TLB)

ENCOURAGEMENT TO FIT

In the fall of 1989, my wife, Evie, and I returned from eight weeks of ministry in Peru. Peru is still in the news today because of the continuing serious problems that we encountered then--runaway inflation, political instability, general unrest, drug traffic, and terror spreading through the cities and the surrounding country. When we flew out of Lima, the country was in a state of emergency.

We could breathe a sigh of relief--but what of those who could not leave? What about the problems which are still present? What message of encouragement is there for such a time? And what hope could we give to the faithful Christian leaders serving there?

I found the perfect words. As God commissioned and installed Joshua for a difficult assignment as Moses' successor, He spoke these words to him: *"Be strong and courageous. Do not be terrified; do not be discouraged: for the Lord your God will be with you wherever you go"* (Joshua 1:9, NIV).

What an amazing text that must have been to Joshua as he inherited this extraordinary assignment from the Lord. This great text seemed perfect and appropriate for our Peruvian coworkers, too. And for you and me in *our* areas of assignment.

DO NOT BE TERRIFIED: God gave these words to Joshua (and us) because He knew how easily *we* are terrified. And He knew we'd often be surrounded by events that could rush fear and anxiety into our lives. Jesus often said, *"Fear not."*

DO NOT BE DISCOURAGED: Again, God gave these words to His followers (then *and* now), knowing our innate tendencies to become discouraged.

We seem to get discouraged for all kinds of reasons: when the "work" is slow and difficult; when the results are meager; when the opposition is stiff; when our health is fragile and breaking; when our relationships with coworkers are strained; when we see poverty, homelessness, and brokenness all around us and we don't know what to do next; when isolation or loneliness gnaws at us; when we are understaffed and overworked.

And we scream, *Who wouldn't be discouraged?*

Read on in the text and notice what God says. After telling Joshua, *Do not be terrified* and *do not be discouraged*, he goes on to say, *"... for the Lord your God will be with you wherever you go."*

Really? Yes, *really*! He has pledged Himself to *always* be with us. Just as He was faithful in His promises to Moses, Joshua, David, His disciples, and Paul--so He will be for you and me.

Yes, even in the fiery furnace times of life. Remember Shadrach, Meshach, and Abednego? The Lord was with them through their experience in the flaming furnace. He was *with them* in the fire!

I wish that I could promise you a trouble-free journey. I'd like to assure you easy ministry assignments with big results, and excellent health with no threat from terrorist organizations. But there are no such promises.

But this I *can* promise you, based on God's Word . . . God will always be with you . . . even in the final moments of life on earth.

> *"Yea, though I walk through the valley of the shadow of death, I will fear no evil; for Thou art with me; thy rod and thy staff they comfort me."*
> Psalm 23:4 (KJV)

ASKING FOR HIS TOUCH

Several years ago while ministering in Africa, I had a free Sunday morning in Nairobi, Kenya. I had been attending a major conference with missionaries from some fifty-two countries around the world. At the conclusion of the conference, I went to the largest evangelical church for a worship service. The church was full (about 4,000) for the second service. The service was alive, warm, and worshipful. Early in the service, the pastor led all of us in singing the familiar, old hymn by Fanny Crosby, *Pass Me Not,* written at least one hundred years ago.

I remember singing this old hymn often as a kid. I had remembered it mainly as an evangelistic hymn to be used during altar calls. But this Sunday, it was different. It was used as a prayer for Christians, asking and inviting God to freshly visit our lives with His touch of *renewal*. I asked God to answer the words of this hymn in my life. In a quiet and simple way, yet personally, pointedly, and powerfully, He met me that morning.

It was a wonderful moment. All of a sudden I was not simply attending another worship service. Not glibly singing an old hymn. Not mouthing words. Not going through the motions. God and I were engaged in mutual encounter. He was deeply ministering to me. I was moved by the warm touch of His love and grace. And I could not hold back the tears as they flowed freely. Here are the words, penned so long ago, that ministered to me that morning:

> Pass me not O gentle Savior; Hear my humble cry;
> While on others Thou art calling, Do not pass me by.
>
> Let me at a throne of mercy Find a sweet relief.
> Kneeling there in deep contrition, Help my unbelief.

Trusting only in Thy merit, Would I seek Thy face;
Heal my wounded broken spirit, Save me by Thy grace.

Thou the spring of all my comfort, More than life to me,
Whom have I on earth beside Thee? Whom in heaven
         but Thee?

(Refrain)
Savior, Savior, hear my humble cry;
While on others Thou art calling, *Do not pass me by.*

Just words? Not really. The words comprise an eloquent prayer. I am praying, right now, that God will not pass you by, but that He will meet you as you invite Him to stop and touch you afresh for the opportunities and challenges that lie ahead. Perhaps you sense a special need. And you are saying, *Lord, I really need you. I want you. Touch me now.*

Perhaps you sense that your need is for renewal . . . for revival . . . for wholeness . . . for forgiveness.

Whatever your need, spend some moments now, bathing yourself in the content of this hymn. Indeed, if you ask, He will not pass you by.

> *"I will not leave you comfortless; I will come to You."*
>
>   John 14:18 (KJV)

> *"Never will I leave you; never will I forsake you."*
>
>   Hebrews 13:56 (NIV)

ALIVE IN CHRIST

God has pledged Himself to always be with us--in good times--in our fiery furnace times--in our ministry assignments--and even **in the final moments of life on earth**. I had written these thoughts in one of our monthly *Encouragement* letters. And these thoughts especially ministered to a friend of mine who wrote to me and later called me, after reflecting on David's confidence expressed in Psalm 23:4. David said, as He pondered God's presence:

> *"Even though I walk through the valley of the shadow of death, I will fear no evil, for you are with me."*

And David added these words of hope and confidence, in verse 6:

> *"Surely goodness and love will follow me all the days of my life and I will dwell in the house of the Lord forever."*

What great words of assurance, hope, and confidence about God's presence *all along the way* . . . with special emphasis on God's presence at the end of the earthly journey.

My friend was especially blessed with this phrase of David, promising His precious presence as we **walk *through* the valley of the shadow of death**. God will not merely lead **us into** the valley and then abandon us. Nor will He simply be with **us in** the valley or wait for us on the other side. He will also lead us **through** the valley. Did you catch the significance of that? This speaks of **entering and exiting** the valley. It suggests that the valley experience is only temporary. Though difficult, perhaps, the valley will not last forever. God will lead us through the valley that separates the temporal from the eternal . . . the mortal from the immortal . . . the corruptible from the incorruptible.

If this is true, and it surely is, then whether we exit temporal life through disease, accident, or even martyrdom, it doesn't matter for God will be with us through the entire process. Remember, death is not termination--it's a *transition* to something beyond our finite understanding. The Apostle Paul adds these words:

> *"To be absent from the body and to be present with the Lord. . . ."*   2 Corinthians 5:8 (KJV)

> *"To live is Christ and to die is gain . . . I desire to depart and be with Christ which is better by far."*
> Philippians 1:21, 23 (NIV)

The Greek construction there literally means that to be with Christ in His heaven is **better, better, better** (a triple comparative).

D.L. Moody said, "Someday you will read in an obituary in the newspaper that D.L. Moody is dead. Don't believe it because at that moment I will be more alive than ever I was here on earth!"

The best is yet to come for all of us who know Christ. He will be with us today and tomorrow . . . and all through the nineties . . . and even the coming new millennium. And when our earthly journey comes to a close, He will be with us *through the valley.*

Ultimately we will be forever with Him in His heaven. Until then, enjoy and practice His presence in your life and ministry.

> *"You will seek me and find me when you seek me with all your heart."*
> Jeremiah 29:13 (NIV)

CONTRASTING HALLS OF FAME

Some time ago, I remember a cover of U.S. NEWS AND WORLD REPORT with this blaring headline: **The Best of America,** and this subtitle: **The Year's Most Outstanding People, Places, Products and Ideas** (July 9, 1990).

My first reaction was, *The best . . . says who?*

I was initially offended by the headline, but I read the rather lengthy article anyway. I was especially interested to read about the "most outstanding people in America." After reading it, I again looked at the cover: **"The Best of America."** Even after several years, I have not yet been able to shake this memory, but in the light of the wider teaching of the Scriptures, I can see these things in a new light.

Who are the most important people in the world? Are they the names listed in the article . . . or the celebrities flashed on CNN, MTV, or other media? Who are the people making the greatest contribution to our lives and our world? And . . . here's an entirely different angle . . . who are the people who ultimately will be in *God's* Hall of Fame?

I immediately thought of many of *you* whom I've met in recent years as I have traveled the world visiting in some ninety countries. What an amazing group of friends I've met who are serving Christ. Some in public positions. Some in hidden places of obscurity. Most serve with absolutely no fanfare and are paid modestly.

Some of you have been told by your friends that you are "wasting your life and could be making a fortune doing something else."

But you have heard the call of God and have made the choice to follow Him. And *you* are making a difference for Christ and

His Kingdom. And from all that I know in the Scriptures, **you are among the most important people.** Those who faithfully follow Him shall be eternally remembered and rewarded by God.

And the magazines with their lists of the "rich and famous," their "brightest" or "most beautiful" and "the best" will end up in the trash. But God's list will last forever.

Malachi wrote these words of encouragement:

> *"Then they that feared the Lord spoke often one to another. And the Lord hearkened and heard it, and a Book of Remembrance was written before Him for them that feared the Lord and that thought upon His Name. And they shall be mine, saith the Lord of hosts, in that day when I make up my jewels."*
> Malachi 3:16-17(KJV)

Did you catch the significance of this text? God is always awake and alert. He is *recording all of our life and ministry* in His Book of Remembrance. Someday, Jesus Christ will return and He will reveal to all of Heaven's hosts (including you and me) just who His special jewels are. I'm convinced that there will be many surprises in that day. The *greatest* individuals will not necessarily be those you and I would have chosen. And certainly not those listed by the *U.S. News and World Report, Time, People* or *Newsweek.* Nor any of the *Who's Who* collections printed yearly around the world.

In your ministry for Jesus Christ, it is *His* assessment that counts. What's written about you in His Book of Remembrance is what ultimately matters.

Your name does not need to be carved in stone in order for you to be counted worthy. You won't need monuments erected to your memory. *God* will remember you.

By the world's standard of measurement, today's heroes are often tomorrow's "*has-beens*." The world is fickle and shallow in its assessment, whether your place is in the field of sports, politics, social service, entertainment, or any career the world places value upon. The Preacher of the Book of Ecclesiastes sums it up best: *"I have seen all the works that are done under the sun; and, behold, all is vanity and vexation of spirit"* (Ecclesiastes 1:14, KJV).

So who are the great ones? Jesus gives us the answer . . . **"He that doeth the will of My Father."**

> Not I, but Christ, be honored, loved, exalted;
> Not I, but Christ, be seen, be known, be heard;
> Not I, but Christ, in every look and action;
> Not I, but Christ, in every thought and word.
>
> Not I, but Christ, in lowly, silent labor;
> Not I, but Christ, in humble, earnest toil;
> Christ, only Christ! no show, no ostentation!
> Christ, only Christ, my All in all to be.
>
> (Refrain)
> Oh, to be saved from myself, dear Lord,
> Oh, to be lost in Thee;
> Oh, that it may be no more I,
> But Christ that lives in me.
> --Mrs. A. A. Whiddington

STUMBLING

Recently, several Christian friends in ministry have fallen . . . and at least temporarily they have been "put on the shelf," away from active ministry. Predictably, I have heard many comments such as:

> "I can't believe it."
> "Isn't it terrible?"
> "How could he so suddenly fall?"

Let's be careful as we see weakness--or failure--or collapse in the life of a fellow servant. The Scriptures tell us NOT to judge one another. NOT to criticize. NOT to strut about with spiritual arrogance . . . *lest we also stumble.*

I should not, and I hope I shall not, judge another . . . for several reasons:

> -Jesus said, *"Judge not, lest you be judged"* (Matthew 7:1).
> -Paul wrote, *"So, if you think you are standing firm, be careful that you don't fall!"* (1 Corinthians 10:12, NIV).
> -I have lived long enough to know my own weaknesses, my own human vulnerabilities, and my own miserable failings.
> -Each of us has the potential for a terrible tumble. That's right, *each of us.* None of us is failure-proof.

For these and other reasons, we need to be sensitive in dealing with brothers and sisters who have struggled and who are struggling.

Last week, a Christian student counselor said to me, "I have observed that when a life is really messed up, usually their personal spiritual life has been grossly neglected."

Dr. Robert Cook, the late President of King's College, said, "Invariably the up and downers, the feeble brothers and sisters who never make the grade for God, are the ones who either willfully or stupidly refuse to make a place and time in their daily schedule for God's Word."

I am not simplistically stating that all problems are automatically and solely due to neglecting our devotional quiet times. I am strongly suggesting, however, that our *spiritual lives will impact every other area of our lives.*

If Bill Clinton, Boris Yeltsin, or Billy Graham invited me to spend a private hour with them, I would drop everything to keep the special appointment. I would accept the invitation. I would prepare for it. I would be prompt. And . . . I would tell everyone about it.

Yet . . . there is Someone even more special who wants private time with you.

One day the apostles of Christ returned from a ministry assignment full of enthusiasm. They were eager to talk about effective ministry. But they were so busy that they weren't even taking time out for leisure. Not even time out to eat. And Jesus said to them, *"Come ye yourselves apart . . . and rest a while"* (Mark 6:31, KJV).

Someone has commented that either we will heed the words of Christ and "come apart" for restoration or we will literally come apart. Either we will know the discipline of spending private time with Christ or we will experience gradual disintegration spiritually . . . and this will possibly be evidenced in moral disintegration. Or we may experience physical disintegration. Maybe emotional disintegration. No one really suddenly stumbles. Rather . . . we slip away. We drift away. Fall away.

Most of us in ministry know the tendency to neglect our spiritual lives. There are plenty of "legitimate" reasons, too. But when we give serious thought to these alibis, we see that they are shallow and insincere.

Even now, Jesus invites you to a private audience with Him. How will you respond?

> *"Whether you turn to the right or to the left, your ears will hear a voice behind you, saying, 'This is the way; walk in it.' "*
>
> Isaiah 30:21 (NIV)

A NEED FOR A LIGHTER GRASP

Amy Carmichael once wrote: *only that which is eternal ultimately matters.* And today . . . these words have new meaning for me.

My wife, Evie, and I recently attended a farm sale. It was an old-fashioned auction at the homestead of Evie's uncle in Minnesota. For 85 years, Victor lived on this farm. All of the buildings were built by his father who came from Sweden one hundred years ago. Because of advancing years, failing eyesight, and ominous health, Victor decided it was time to sell and move to town.

I suppose the sale went well. But it was difficult for all of us in the family. Nostalgic? Yes. Traumatic? Yes. During the auction, I often stole a glance at Uncle Victor. I am sure he had jumbled emotions as he saw all of his possessions auctioned to the highest bidder. *Sold!* Gone . . . probably never to be seen again.

Hundreds of items were sold. Like the two trunks that his parents had brought over from Sweden. And the wooden wheelbarrow that his brother, Albin, had made. And the tools his dad had made. Also gone--the tractor . . . the pickup truck . . . the old wood stove.

In a few days, Victor will be off to a new life in a town close by. And before long, he will be moving onward--upward--to yet better things prepared by God for those who know Him and love Him.

I was reminded of the transitory nature of all things. Stuart Hamblen's poetry came to mind:

> "the things of earth will dim and lose their value,
> when we recall they're borrowed for a while . . . "

Indeed, everything on earth is transitory. All of our possessions are just "borrowed for a while." The place we once called home will someday cease to be our home. Today's "new" car will soon be outdated and useless--our possessions will belong to someone else.

I realize that we must hold **things** lightly. Abraham understood this as he *"made his home in the promised land like a stranger in a foreign country . . . looking forward to the city with foundations, whose architect and builder is God"* (Hebrews 10: 9-10, NIV).

Paul wrote, *"Now we know that if the earthly tent we live in is destroyed, we have a building from God, an eternal house in heaven, not built by human hands"* (2 Corinthians 5:1, NIV).

Jesus added to this, *"Lay not up for yourselves treasures upon the earth where moth and rust destroy, and where thieves break in and steal but store up for yourselves treasures in heaven, where moth and rust do not destroy, and where thieves do not break in and steal"* (Matthew 6:19-20, NIV).

My friend, are you sometimes longing for *things*? Are you sometimes confused about where *home* is? Do you linger over thoughts about your kids and their status? Is the body beginning to wear down? Are you getting anxious for Heaven? All of these things remind us that we are here on earth briefly. We are *in transit*. And we are surrounded by transitory things. So let us keep a light touch on things about us and let us keep a *firm grasp on that which is eternal*. We're "heading home" to a beautiful city, a permanent home, and perfected bodies. *The best is yet to be!*

> Nothing between my soul and the Saviour,
> Naught of this world's delusive dream;
> I have renounced all sinful pleasure,
> Jesus is mine; there's nothing between.
> --Chas. A. Tindley

THE FRUIT OF ANGUISH

Weekly we receive letters from servants in ministry from all over the world. Some come from friends or acquaintances. Often we hear from total strangers who frequently share personal times of turmoil and struggle. For example:

> One woman wrote of a "dark valley of illness" and identified her disease as a type of malaria which was resistant to most medications. Yet later, after a long and painful struggle with the disease, she was restored to health. She wrote, "The entire experience was worth it. Through it all, a friend came to Christ."

Another person wrote of spending time with a dying relative. He shared one of our letters of *Encouragement* and saw his loved one find confidence and assurance as he passed from physical life--through death--to *real life*, in Christ.

And another person wrote these painful thoughts: "I returned from the field burned out and feeling like I'd failed. My adjustment to all of this has not been easy. But finally I am beginning to feel alive again."

Problems and pressures are all around us. Overseas and here at home, also. You can probably add to the situations mentioned above . . . financial disasters . . . family disappointments . . . broken dreams . . . relational conflicts. In fact, why don't you list the thing or things with which you are now burdened.

The pressing question always is this. *How do I respond in the difficult moments of life? How do I emerge as a victor instead of as a victim?*

The other day I was reading from Isaiah 38 about King Hezekiah. The text says that Hezekiah was ill . . . to the point of death. God had told him he had an illness from which he would not recover. As you might imagine, this news sent the king into despair. He pleaded with God for an extension of life and God granted the king another fifteen years. Here is what King Hezekiah said in response to God's gift of added years and reflecting on his personal anguish:

> *"I will walk humbly all of my years because of this* ***anguish*** *of my soul."*   (Isaiah 38:15)

> *"Surely it was for my benefit that I suffered such* ***anguish.***"   (Isaiah 38:17)

Did you notice that the king mentioned his trial two times and both times referred to it as *anguish*? That word, in Hebrew, is a very intense word. The king's problem was enormous. It was *heavy*. But in retrospect, the king recognized that the experience had been good for him. It had positive benefits. The results were good.

Most of us, in retrospect, can see that God brings *good* out of bitter times. Our greater difficulty is dealing with the anguish *at the time of the anguish*. The immensity of emotion and heaviness of our feelings usually obscure our vision of God's purposes for us. Yet, it's during this *actual time of the anguish* that we must learn to trust God. Even through tears, uncertainty, and great perplexity . . . we must place our trust *totally* in our dependable Heavenly Father.

> *". . . the Spirit helps us in our weakness. We do not know what we ought to pray, but the Spirit himself intercedes for us with groans that words cannot express. . . . And we know that in all things God works together for the good of those who love Him, who have been called according to His purpose."*
>
> Romans 8:26, 28 (TLB)

THE LANGUAGE OF FORGIVENESS

I recall the greetings from the beautiful country of Papua New Guinea where the language, *Tok Pisin*, is spoken and understood by most of the masses of people. It is a great language . . . a fun language . . . an expressive language.

> *"**BLUT** BILONG JISAS PIKININI BILONG GOD, EM I SAVE **TEKEWE** OLGETA SIN BILONG YUMI NA YUMI KAMAP **KLIN"** (1 John 1:7).*

And in my memory, I am looking at a bark banner with the above verse quoted and painted on its rough texture. One of the English translations of the verse reads like this . . .

> *"The blood of Jesus, his Son, purifies us from all sin."*

But the actual New Guinea Pidgin translation is richer--somehow easier to grasp in its freshness. Literally it is translated like this . . .

> *"The Blood that belongs to Jesus, the Son belonging to God, takes away (TEKEWE) all sin that belongs to us (YUMI) and we (YUMI) come up clean (KAMAP KLIN)."*

More smoothly, yet still accurately, it reads . . .

> *"The Blood of Jesus, God's Son, takes away (TEKEWE) all of our sin and we come up clean (KAMAP KLIN)."*

This dynamic truth is intellectually known to most of us; still, it may be that it is appreciated and experienced by *too few of us*. Indeed our theology affirms that through the blood of Christ, at Calvary, we were forgiven, as we trusted Christ for our salvation.

In addition to this fact accomplished by the sacrifice of the Lord, the blood of Christ *continues to work* for us *day and night forever*, cleansing us from our *past, present, and future* sins.

The Biblical text tells us that as we confess our sins, walking in the light, **God is forgiving us.** Take another look at the Pidgin text, sounding out the words. As a result of His blood at work in our lives, two things are happening now--in the *present.*

Our sins are taken away. That means that God not only forgives us all of our confessed sins, but He also forgets all of our sins.

That's the truth . . . *forgiven* and *forgotten.* Hear the truth variously stated in the Scriptures . . .

> *"As far as the east is from the west, so far hath he removed our transgressions from us."*
> (Psalm 103:12, KJV)

> Isaiah says that God *". . . hast cast my sins behind thy back"* and will never look at them again.
> (Isaiah 38:17, KJV)

> *"Thou wilt cast all their sins into the depths of the sea."* (Micah 7:19, NASB)

> **We come up clean.** What a wonderful word. What an encouraging word. **Clean.** Even though the sin was hideous, **Clean.** Even though the sin was ugly, **Clean.** Even though the sin was gross, **Clean!**

Indeed, sometimes I find it hard to accept this and believe it. I often do not feel that I deserve this gift from God. Sometimes I feel so dirty that even after confession, I *do not feel clean.* But the truth is that *I am forgiven*. God says so in English, in Tok Pisin, in Spanish, in Russian, and in the language of His Spirit.

Maybe Satan has hassled you too long and kept you in the pit of despair over past sin. Perhaps because of the habit of recurring sins. Or the guilt-ridden anguish of hidden sins. But hear it now--believe it now--shout it now. ***By His grace and through the blood of Christ, He has taken my sin away. I am forgiven. I come up clean. Praise God!***

Marvelous grace of our loving Lord,
Grace that exceeds our sin and our guilt,
Yonder on Calvary's mount outpoured,
There where the blood of the Lamb was spilt.

Marvelous, infinite, matchless grace,
Freely bestowed on all who believe;
You that are longing to see His face,
Will you this moment His grace receive?

(Refrain)
Grace, grace, God's grace,
Grace that will pardon and cleanse within;
Grace, grace, God's grace,
Grace that is greater than all our sin.
                                        --Julia H. Johnston

LENIN AND JESUS

En route from Peru to the United States, I had just finished reading the day's issue of **USA Today**. I was blessed by one article. Blessed? . . . *by reading the daily newspaper?* Yes.

The paper reported on a new public opinion poll taken in the Soviet Union which revealed that 58% of those polled believed that in the year 2000, Jesus Christ will be the Man with the greatest influence on Soviet life. The poll specifically predicted that His influence would be greater than that of either Lenin or Gorbachev.

I sat back in my airplane seat in amazement. What an incredible statistic coming out of a nation which since 1917 has officially embraced atheism as the official religion of the country. The communist government did everything it could to eliminate Christianity from the system. But now after more than 75 years, the majority of the people--according to **USA Today**--sees not only the failure of communism and atheism but the growing influence of Jesus Christ in their country and in their lives. Remarkable!

Earlier that same year, I had the privilege of preaching in the Soviet Union, and I can affirm firsthand the hunger of the people for information about Jesus. We distributed 16,000 copies of the Scriptures to people . . . including soldiers and policemen. Others also were eagerly grasping for copies of this Book telling about history's most significant Character . . . Jesus Christ. Born almost 2,000 years ago . . . in a small village . . . He was forever destined to change the world by changing the lives of people.

Since His birth, many others have entered our world and been on the stage of human history briefly. There have been many "great" ones including kings, presidents, political leaders, philosophers, educators, etc. Many have captured the headlines. Some have made quite a stir. Some have been luminaries for a moment and others for a much longer time. Still, all have or will fade away dramatically compared to this One very special Life. Bill Gaither says it well . . . *"Kings and Kingdoms will all pass away but there's something about HIS NAME."*

The Apostle Paul writes . . .

> *"God highly exalted Him and bestowed on Him the Name which is above every name, that at the Name of Jesus every knee should bow, of those who are in heaven, and on earth, and under the earth, and that every tongue should confess that Jesus Christ is Lord, to the Glory of God the Father."*
>
> Philippians 2:9-11 (NASB)

In another text Paul refers to Jesus as the *Preeminent One* (Colossians 1:18). Another translation states it like this . . . *That in all things He might come to have **First Place**.*

Sometimes it may not look like Jesus will be the ultimate Victor. Often it seems that our world is out of control. But the final chapter has been written and will someday be played out in history. Jesus will indeed have *first place* in everything. Not only as Lord over history. Not just as Lord over all humanity. But Lord of *all*.

May it be so even now in our lives as we give to Him a renewed commitment and have Him Lord over our personal life and ministry. He will be universally acknowledged as *King of kings and Lord of lords*, and through all eternity it will forever be so.

> All hail the power of Jesus' name!
> Let angels prostrate fall;
> Bring forth the royal diadem,
> And crown Him Lord of all!
> --Edward Perronet

DO NOT FEAR

Let's consider **FEAR** for a few moments.

Some time ago, Evie and I were invited to spend a few hours in conversation with mission friends in Latin America. Each of them was assigned for ministry in a location that was terrorist-prone. They asked if we'd lead a retreat with emphasis on handling *fear*.

At that time, the world stood on the brink of war in the Middle East. Indeed, war did break out between Allied Forces and Iraq. And perhaps you recall the waves of *fear* that were unleashed worldwide as we watched reports on CNN of Scud missiles, threatened biological weapons and bombing raids.

You and I can add to these illustrations all of our own fears. Anxiety from past failures that still linger close by. Fears of our present concerns--anxious thoughts of our kids, our aging parents, our financial resources, our retirement, our difficult relationships with fellow workers, our health. The list of real fears is endless. No doubt, you could add your own personal fears.

The Scriptures have much to say about fear. David candidly speaks of fear in his own life. I am especially impressed with the string of difficulties mentioned in Psalm 55 and Psalm 56--*anguish, terrors of death, fear and trembling, horror, and distress.* David also longs to escape and says, *"Oh that I had the wings of a dove. I would fly away and be at rest."*

David gives us help in handling fear. He says: *"When I am afraid, I will trust in Thee . . . in whose word I praise, in God I have put my trust; I shall not be afraid"* (Psalm 56:3-4, NASB).

Not **IF** *I am afraid*, but **WHEN** *I am afraid*. Like David, you and I will *often* be afraid. And when fear comes, we may find ourselves preoccupied and immobilized by it. Intimidated with it. Even destroyed by it. But the Scriptures say that David took specific action when fear came into his life. He did two things:

1. **When David was afraid he *trusted* God** (Psalm 56: 3, 11).

   To trust God is to take decisive action by placing full confidence in Him, even when circumstances are brutal and your understanding is minimal. Job, when stripped of almost everything, proclaimed, *Even though He slay me, yet will I trust in the Lord.* Perhaps we will find ourselves, through tear-filled eyes, affirming our trust in the Lord. "Lord, I don't know what's going on--but I know You--and I know that *You* know what's happening in my life. I can trust You." *Make the conscious choice to trust God.*

2. **When David was afraid he *praised* God** (Psalm 56: 4, 10).

   Toward the end of the Book of Psalms, there is a rising crescendo of praise. David learned to praise God. And we must learn to praise Him. This isn't our natural inclination. Rather, praise is a *learned response* to fear. Even when we do not *feel* like praising God, it's still the proper, godly response. It's always appropriate to praise God--even healthy--to learn to sing the Doxology when we are afraid.

As I write these words, I'm writing them to myself. My heart needs to learn to respond to fear as did David . . . by trusting God and by praising God. Let's begin to practice these responses to our fears.

> *"For God did not give us a spirit of timidity, but a spirit of power, of love and of self-discipline."*
> 2 Timothy 1:7 (NIV)

THE BLESSING

Did you know that all of God's people are called to the ministry of blessing? Specifically, we are called to *bless one another*. In fact, this principle is clearly stated frequently in the Scriptures. The idea appears early in the Old Testament and toward the end of the New Testament:

1. God called Abraham and his descendents to such a ministry in Genesis 12:2: *"I will bless you and you will be a blessing."* The English rendering of this seems a bit vague. In the Hebrew, however, it is clear that God was giving an exhortation to His people. They were called to bless each other. It was a divine command.

2. Peter, the Apostle, in 1 Peter 3:9, issues the call again. *"Bless one another, because to this you were called so that you may inherit a blessing."* This text also seems to indicate that there is a "boomerang effect" attached to blessing one another. As we bless, we will be blessed. Blessing begets blessing.

Do we do as well as we can in fulfilling this great expectation to bless others? We frequently say to each other, "God bless you." And that's appropriate. Indeed all blessing *does* come from Him. But He also makes us partners with Him. So often His blessing is communicated through human agents--people to people. Wonderful. We have the potential of blessing each other. But there are lots of questions about this--why, who, where, and how?

Why should we bless one another? That's an easy question to answer. *Because God tells us to do it.*

Who should we bless? There are no limits here. We are called to bless generously. Let it come consciously, deliberately, and freely.

111

Parents to children, and children to parents. Husbands to wives, and wives to husbands. Neighbors to neighbors. Missionaries to missionaries. And even blessings to strangers. In fact, the Bible says, *"Do not forget to entertain strangers, for by so doing some people have entertained angels without knowing it"* (Hebrews 13:2, NIV).

Where should we bless? Again, let there be no limits. Let's make this a daily priority--in the family, on the job, on the mission center, at the marketplace, on the train--in fact, everywhere we go. But more specifically, let us bless one another in familiar friendships. In prolonged relationships. And yes, even in brief encounters. Possibly even in anonymous encounters. The Book of Acts states that when Peter walked through the city of Jerusalem, *even his shadow brought blessing to all that it fell upon.* Amazing, isn't it? I pray that my life will bring such blessing as I journey through each day.

How should we bless one another? There are a number of suggestions:

>1. Through a radiant face, reflecting the inner joy of the indwelling Christ. A friend of mine has often prayed, "Lord, give me a radiant face."

>2. Through words of encouragement and hope.

>3. Through a "meaningful touch," to quote Smalley and Trent in their excellent book, *The Blessing.* Let's not be afraid of a touch . . . a hug . . . an embrace.

>4. Through sharing a thought from the Bible, which calls itself *The Book of Encouragement.*

I recall a familiar hymn from childhood. The refrain of this lovely old song is actually a prayer, which is my prayer for today, tomorrow, and for the rest of my journey. Will you also adopt this prayer for your life?

> Out of the highways and byways of life,
> Many are weary and sad;
> Carry the sunshine where darkness is rife,
> Making the sorrowing glad.
>
> Give as 'twas given to you in your need,
> Love as the Master loved you;
> Be to the helpless a helper indeed,
> Unto your mission be true.
>
> (Refrain)
> Make me a blessing, make me a blessing,
> Out of my life, may Jesus shine;
> Make me a blessing, O Saviour, I pray,
> Make me a blessing to someone today.
>
> --Ira B. Wilson

THE VALUE OF PAIN

Recently, I made a visit to my photographer, a fine Christian friend. He's a husband and father with two young children. The conversation was inspirational and memorable. He told me of his bout with lymphatic cancer and his present apparent wholeness of health. Together we thanked God for His mercy. Then my friend said to me with deep feeling and sincerity, "My cancer experience was the best thing that ever happened to me."

The best thing that ever happened? Strange use of the word *"best."* I recall the usage of that word *best* in similar circumstances. Martin Luther said, "The best book in my library is the book called affliction." Charles Spurgeon, in considering those words by Luther added this thought: ". . . and the best page in that book of affliction is the blackest page of all."

Interestingly, many people cannot even *begin* to comprehend such things. *Most men and women without Christ do not understand this.* And even some Christians have trouble with the concept of wedding goodness to affliction--joy and pain.

We've all come to know through experience that there are no guarantees that we will ever live trouble-free here on this earth. No one can get through life without trouble. Not unbelievers. Not Christians. Even those of us who are involved in ministry and missions are not exempt. In fact, the opposite is true.

Jesus told His followers, *". . . in this world you will have trouble"* (John 16:33, NIV). And as another reminder, the Apostle Paul wrote to his young protege, *"Yea, and all that will live godly in Christ Jesus shall suffer . . . "* (2 Timothy 3:12, KJV).

But can life's darkest hours be called the *best* hours of all? My photographer would say, "Yes!" Martin Luther would certainly agree.   So would Charles Spurgeon.   And our Old Testament friend, Job, would undoubtedly concur.   After he was stripped of his health, his wealth, his family, and his friends, Job saw only the Lord.   And he heard only the voice of the Lord.

As God spoke to Job in warm, personal, intimate and powerful words, something profound happened to Job.   Job's perspective on his trials changed.   He saw beauty emerge out of ashes.   It's hard to imagine our own response to God in similar circumstances.

Job said to the Lord, *"Once my ears had heard of you but now my eyes have seen you"* (Job 42:5, NIV).   Let me paraphrase that verse.   Job was saying, *"Through my affliction, O Lord, I have **really seen You.** Now I **really** know You."*

Job is saying that he came to know God's sufficiency as reality, not mere theory.   Job found the Lord's promises to be *utterly reliable*:

> *God's strength is really sufficient. He does give strength for each day. He does give songs in the night. When you walk through the valley of the shadow of death, He will be with you.*

Even in *your* present trial, God has a *hidden blessing* for you.   There is a beautiful benefit in your time of trauma.   Even in the deepest valley, He stands ready to bless you. ***Out of your "worst" times can come your "best" experiences.***

> *"Though You have made me see troubles, many and bitter, You will restore my life again; from the depths of the earth You will again bring me up."*
> Psalm 71:20 (NIV)

DON'T SAY EVERYTHING

Several days ago I picked up the in-house bulletin of a hotel I was visiting. One of the articles was entitled "Communication . . . Getting Along With People." The article was excellent. The first guideline stopped me in my tracks. Here it is: *"Don't say everything you think."*

Obviously many people do not follow this guideline. Even we Christians are not necessarily committed to this. Some rather think we ought "to tell it like it is." Some constantly trumpet the passage from Ephesians 4:15, which says, *"Speak the truth in love . . . ,"* assuming this gives us permission to *say everything we think.*

Few Scriptural texts are more misused and abused than this one. This text does not give us permission to bang each other over the head with verbal baseball bats. *It does not invite us to say everything we think.* Not at all.

Often I have had regrets over something I have said to another friend, associate, or family member. I think to myself, "I wish I hadn't said that." The maturing Christian should have a growing sensitivity about the use of speech toward others.

You've probably noticed that the Bible has a lot to say about our speech. You could probably spend extensive time in James 3 or in the Book of Proverbs, especially noting all that is said about the *tongue.* We have the potential of blessing or cursing with our tongues . . . building up or tearing down . . . helping or hurting . . . encouraging or discouraging.

Reflect on these ideas from God's Word on the theme of speech:

"The tongue has the power of life and death."
(Proverbs 18:21)

"Everyone should be quick to listen, slow to speak."
(James 1:19)

"The lips of the righteous know what is fitting."
(Proverbs 10:32)

"Do not let any unwholesome talk come out from your mouths, but only what is helpful for building others up according to their needs, that it may benefit those who listen."
(Ephesians 4:29)

"The tongue that brings healing is a tree of life."
(Proverbs 15:4)

"A word aptly spoken is like apples of gold in settings of silver."   (Proverbs 25:12)

So again . . . **don't say everything you think.** Because it's *not always necessary.* And it may not be helpful. It may not be healing. Nor edifying.

But, you ask, how can I change? How can I help myself and show more self-control? The truth is, you and I *do not have the power* to control our tongues. But, thankfully . . . *God can control our tongues.* We need His help. We *need* Spirit-controlled tongues.

What a difference this could make in our relationships in our homes, our churches, our play centers, and in our workplace. David often made this prayer his prayer:

"Set a guard over my mouth, O Lord: keep watch over the door of my life."
Psalm 141: 3 (NIV)

117

DIFFICULT AND WONDERFUL

As I was traveling in my car some mornings ago, I heard a taped message by Luci Swindoll. She began with two comments and then proceeded to amplify both points. Here are the two general statements:

Life is difficult
Life is wonderful

Ever since hearing the message, I have pondered the meaning of each statement individually and the relationship of these two statements. Initially, they sound mutually exclusive, yet both are true and Biblically sound. And, yes, both *can* live and coexist in our lives and experience--and more particularly in our approach to life. In fact, both *must* exist *in balance* within us in order for life to truly make sense.

Life is difficult.

Immediately I hear you saying, "Amen!" We are all convinced, from our own experience, that life *is* difficult--very difficult. Everyone has an abundance of problems, personal heartaches, financial pressures, broken relationships, misunderstood friendships, unrelenting temptations, shattered dreams, unrealistic expectations--and, well, you can fill in the blank.

From our own experiences and that of our friends, we know that life is indeed difficult. Murphy's Law (if anything can go wrong, it will go wrong) has been operative in all of our lives and ministries. (And if Murphy's Law is not serious enough, you can add Lindquist's Law, which states that *Murphy was an optimist!*)

Somehow it is helpful to know that life is and will continue to be difficult. We ought to accept the fact that difficulties will always be present with us.

Jesus said, *"In this world you will have trouble."*
(John 16:33, NIV)

Peter said, *"Do not be surprised at the painful trial you are suffering."* (1 Peter: 4:12)

Yet we *are* often surprised with our troubles. We always wonder, "Why me?" We get disillusioned; sometimes we even become embittered.

But I have learned through experience that it is better for us to **expect and accept** the inevitability of troubles and reverses along the way. In fact, I believe it is *necessary* for me to *expect life to be difficult.* But that is *only one side of the coin.*

Life is also wonderful.

Every day has its special moments. Every trial has its hidden blessings. We are surrounded by goodness and beauty. We need to learn to look for the presence of God throughout the day. We need to state and sing the Biblical refrain: *"This is the day that the Lord has made. Let us rejoice and be glad in it."*

Some years ago I heard a powerful Christian businessman give a motivational message to a group of business people. The speaker, Charles "Tremendous" Jones, would often kick up his heels during his speech and state, *"Life is tremendous!"*

He really *believed* it. Life was exciting and tremendous. And his positive and optimistic attitude was infectious to all of us who listened to him. We believed it, too.

Yes--life is difficult *and* life is wonderful.

I am finding it important to live with the reality of both of these truths vibrating within me. Often the writers of the Scriptures wedded the two thoughts together within a singular context:

Jesus spoke of *trouble and peace* (John 16:33).

Peter spoke of *blessedness and sufferings* (1 Peter 4:16).

Paul wrote from a prison cell and referred to his *chains*,
and yet the theme of that Philippian epistle is *joy* . . .
(Philippians 1)

Thank you, Luci, for calling us to a balanced approach to life's difficulties and also to the joy and wonder of it all.

"Consider it pure joy, my brothers, whenever you face trials of many kinds, because you know that the testing of your faith develops perseverance. Perseverance must finish its work so that you may be mature and complete, not lacking anything. . . . Blessed is the man who perseveres under trial, because he will receive the crown of life that God has promised to those who love Him."
James 1:2-4, 12 (TLB)

FORGIVENESS

An anonymous author has penned these words:

> If our greatest need had been information--God would have sent us an educator.
> If our greatest need had been technology--God would have sent us a scientist.
> If our greatest need had been money--God would have sent us an economist.
> If our greatest need had been pleasures--God would have sent us an entertainer.
> But our greatest need was forgiveness--So God sent us a Savior.

God knew exactly what we needed most and He responded to this great need when He sent us Jesus Christ, the Savior. Even before His birth, an angel announced the purpose of His visit to Joseph: *"You are to give Him the name Jesus because He will save His people from their sins"* (Matthew 1:21, NIV).

FORGIVENESS . . . THE MESSAGE THAT WE PROCLAIM

> Peter, at Pentecost, proclaimed Jesus' forgiveness: *"Repent and be baptized, every one of you, in the name of Jesus Christ for the forgiveness of your sins"* (Acts 2:38, NIV).

> Paul and Barnabas, in Antioch, had the same message. *"I want you to know that through Jesus the forgiveness of sins is proclaimed to you"* (Acts 13:38, NIV).

The Good News that we proclaim is still relevant after 2,000 years. Jesus Christ is still the central theme of our Gospel and in Him individuals find abundant and eternal life, peace, joy, purpose, heaven, and forgiveness. We continue to affirm that Jesus Christ is also the *only* Source of salvation.

It's been my privilege to proclaim this message all over the world. And I've seen lives changed as they have responded to the message of this Gospel. After meeting Jesus and hearing His words, *"you are forgiven,"* they have begun a new life.

FORGIVENESS--THE PROMISE THAT WE EXPERIENCE

As believers, God's forgiveness continues as a most significant encouragement to *us*. Jesus **did** pay for our sins at the cross, once and for all. And our forgiveness is related to that event. Indeed, Jesus **did** forgive us at the time of our conversion. When we accepted Christ, His forgiveness was personalized to our accounts. But there is something more here. Jesus also *forgives us now*.

Since accepting Christ, we struggle "toward the mark." We never quite arrive, spiritually. It's an ongoing effort. If we think we are without sin--if we think we are now sinless--we are only fooling ourselves. Because of this, we still need cleansing and forgiveness to enjoy fellowship with the Father. But John also gives us this wonderful promise:

> *"If we confess our sins, He is faithful and just to forgive us our sins and to cleanse us from all unrighteousness."*   1 John 1:9 (KJV)

The blood of Jesus Christ *continues to work for us* day and night to make us clean. So, claim this promise. And enjoy His forgiveness.

> *"I am ready for anything through the strength of the One who lives within me."*
>   Philippians 4:10 (PHILLIPS)

R.I.P. LENIN

Evie and I returned from my third trip to Eastern Europe in sixteen months. Each trip had been encouraging . . . really incredible. Doors opened for the message of the Gospel and for aggressive Christian ministry. For those of us who had grown up during several generations of the Cold War, it was all the more remarkable to watch a formerly atheistic regime collapse and give way to the Christian message.

The most recent trip included ministry stops in Hungary, Romania, and in the Soviet Union--Moldavia, the Ukraine, and Russia. The key cities we visited were Budapest, Cluj, Kishnev, former Odessa, Kiev, Bravory, and Moscow. Our time was spent with pastors, church leaders, and seminary professors. I had the joy of preaching Christ in absolute liberty.

My key question for these brethren in Christ, on behalf of the Board of Barnabas International, was this: Is there anything that Barnabas International can or should do with the new era of openness in the Soviet Union and other parts of Eastern Europe? I was convinced that God would have *all* believers grasp this moment. *What an amazing moment in human history!*

Speaking of Open Doors--the opportunities were--and still are--absolutely overwhelming:

> Open Doors for ***Bible Distribution***--they need millions of copies.
> Open Doors for ***Evangelism***--including open air meetings and opportunities, schools, prisons, churches, etc.
> Open Doors for ***Church Planting***--as new believers look for a fellowship of other Christians to help them grow.

Open Doors for *Lay Training and Equipping*--the growing number of Christian leaders and workers.

Open Doors for *Outside Help from Christians*--all over the world.

I'm reminded of Jesus' words in the first century to the church in Philadelphia (Revelation 3): *"I have placed before you an open door that no man can close."* Again in these closing years of the twentieth century, these same words of Jesus speak to His Church with contemporary vitality and truth.

Two scenes of that trip are especially embedded in my memory. I think they tell the present-day story of the former Soviet Union:

1. The Statues/Monuments of Lenin Are Coming Down

All over Eastern Europe the monuments and symbols of Communism are being dismantled. Specifically, we stood in the major square of Kiev, the capital of the Ukraine, and watched the enormous crane begin the process of removing the huge, marble Lenin monument. Yes, we saw the first few stones removed in a process that would take many days. But the destruction of such universal symbolism is charged with emotion and zeal.

2. The Cross of Christ Is Being Lifted Up

One Saturday afternoon in Odessa as we familiarized ourselves with the city, we noticed scaffolding on top of a large dome of a Russian Orthodox Church. During the last seven decades (the lifetime of most people), many churches have been used as museums, schools, warehouses, and the like--certainly not places of worship. Yet all of that is changing now. The governments are returning former church buildings that were confiscated during the

Communist revolution back to congregations as more and more Christians request places for worship.

Oh, yes--remember the scaffolding? The next day, Sunday, as we again drove by this Orthodox Church, a large Cross of Christ had been re-erected on the dome, and the scaffolding was being removed. We had goose bumps. The cameras were clicking. We were praising God. Can you believe this dramatic change?

That's the story. The statues of Lenin are coming down and the Cross of Christ is being lifted up.

Doors that were once closed *are open.* Let's never forget that *God is in the business of opening doors.* And when He does, let's be there to claim the territory for the Lord.

> O where are kings and empires now
> Of old that went and came?
> But, Lord, Thy Church is praying yet,
> A thousand years the same.
>
> For not like kingdoms of the world
> Thy Holy Church, O God;
> Though earthly shocks do threaten her,
> And tempests are abroad.
>
> Unshaken as eternal hills,
> Immovable she stands;
> A mountain that shall fill the earth;
> A house not made with hands.
>   --A. Cleveland Coxe

PRAYER IS HARD WORK

Oswald Chambers wrote these words about prayer:

> *Prayer does not fit us for the greater works;*
> *prayer **is** the greater work.*

If more of us really believed this, we would decisively make prayer a major part of our lives. We would rearrange our daily agendas for the purpose of scheduling prolonged periods of prayer.

I had completed three weeks of ministry in India as part of a preaching team, where Dr. Wesley Duewel and I shared in prayer conferences for pastors and Christian leaders. A third member of the team, Rev. Charles Elkjer, was the resident intercessor. It was Dr. Duewel's goal to call the church of India to the priority of prayer. He had previously spent 25 years in that country as a missionary. He has INDIA written on his heart.

Dr. Duewel wanted to make yet another significant impact on India so accepted the invitation to host major conferences in five areas of the country. The conferences were well attended. There were messages on the subject of prayer but probably more important-- there were opportunities for demonstrating the truth and power of prayer through *actual sessions of praying* during these conferences.

Dr. Duewel, author of *Touch the World Through Prayer* and *Ablaze for God,* is truly a man of prayer. Powerful prayer. I learned much from what he said, but more from his life. He reminded me of Epaphras, about whom Paul wrote, *"Epaphras is always wrestling in prayer for you"* (Colossians 4:12). Often the three of us prayed together. And frequently I'd observe these men in prayer--while walking--while lying on the bed--while sitting in the worship service. I found myself often longing for this quality of prayer discipline in my own life and asking God, "Lord, teach *me* to pray." Never before had I sensed such a need for a deeper *personal prayer life*. Never had I sensed the *enormous potential* of intercessory prayer. Never did I understand the potential of going *deeper into prayer*, from ASKING, to SEEKING, to KNOCKING.

Perhaps you, too, are sensing a need to move deeper into your prayer experience with the Lord. Then again, maybe you *haven't* given it serious thought. After all, you spend time in prayer. You ask, "Is there such a need in the lives of pastors or missionaries?" Yes. Evidently so. The disciples sensed such a need when they asked Jesus to teach them to pray. Later, the leaders of the Early Church (in the Book of Acts) sensed the need. They simplified their schedules and even eliminated some of their activities so that they could give priority to the Word and to prayer (Acts 6:4).

Sometimes I feel that we have come up with a lot of "good" things that have kept us from the *best*--PRAYER. We are busy--but not PRAYERFUL. We've worked to build reputations as excellent preachers, translators, or administrators, but we've not valued the real importance of pursuing the ministry of intercession.

Believe me, I am writing to myself.

> ". . . *in everything by prayer and supplication with thanksgiving, let your requests be made known to God.*"
>
> Philippians 4:6 (KJV)

> ". . . *my God shall supply all your needs according to His riches in glory by Christ Jesus.*"
>
> Philippians 4:19 (KJV)

HOW TO CARRY CHAINS

How are you handling your *"chains of affliction"*? More about that in a minute.

One night I watched Joni Eareckson Tada give her testimony on a Billy Graham television program. I was deeply moved to watch her radiant face and to hear her victorious story. Her story is remarkable, but it's even more inspiring to see Joni sharing it from her confinement in a wheelchair.

Most of us have heard Joni's story, read her book, and seen her movie. But if you haven't met her through one of these, let me refresh your memory. As a teenager, Joni was swimming with friends when she dove into shallow water of Chesapeake Bay. She struck bottom and was instantly made a quadriplegic.

But now, years later, God is using her in a worldwide ministry to people. I have heard her speak of her injury as a *gift from God*. Joni says that she probably would never have had such an extensive and persuasive ministry *without her injury*. She has learned to serve God effectively ***because of her handicap*** and not ***in spite of her handicap***.

Some days after watching Joni on TV, I received a brief note from Dave Dravecky, a former starting pitcher with the San Francisco Giants.   Dave had just finished his baseball career. Following a series of physical problems with his pitching arm, the doctors tried all sorts of medical solutions to help Dave, but were not successful.   Reluctantly, Dave's doctors were forced to surgically remove his arm because of a spreading malignancy.

And of course, that meant an end to his illustrious baseball career. Dave's note to me said, "Thank you for your recent expression of prayers are very important to my family and me. Things are progressing according to God's timing for His plan. It is a blessing to feel the manifestation of His love through you."

And in the time since the arm amputation, God is using and magnifying Dave's ministry in a powerful manner *because of his physical crisis*.

Again, how are you handling your chains? In Philippians 1, Paul mentions his "chains" three times, referring to his prison experience. His chains were beyond his control. Paul *did not choose* his chains. He would probably have avoided them if possible. But repeatedly he speaks of the benefits, blessings, and open doors for ministry that came to him *because of his chains* (Philippians 1:14). Paul's overwhelming goal was to serve God. The issue of his chains was incidental.

All of us have chains of one sort or another. Most of us have some kind of a handicap. It might not be the same kind of "chains" of the Apostle Paul--or of Joni--or of Dave. But there is *something* that can *hinder or limit* your life and ministry.

And you desperately want those chains to be *removed*. You honestly feel that if the chains that bind you could be removed, then you could be unleashed for greater ministry. Well--not necessarily. God might want to use you dynamically and creatively *with* your chains. Have you ever considered that option?

There might be the beginning of a brand new chapter of real effectiveness through your life and ministry--*because of your "chains."*

So--getting back to my initial query . . . *how are you handling your chains?*

Too often, and too quickly, I see my own chains as hindering my work . . . limiting my effectiveness . . . perhaps even silencing my ministry. That's because I'm afraid we're prone to look at things from a *human perspective* and *not from God's point of view*.

Satan hopes that you will get so discouraged with your chains that you will "throw in the towel"--maybe even get angry or bitter with God. But God has a better idea. In your weakness, He can display His strength--and in the process, *your ministry could be maximized for His glory*.

> *"And He said unto me, My grace is sufficient for thee; for My strength is made perfect in weakness. Most gladly therefore will I rather glory in my infirmities, that the power of Christ may rest upon me."*
>
> 2 Corinthians 12:9 (KJV)

FALLING ON OUR FACES

A disturbing statistic was reported by Dr. Arch Hart of Fuller Seminary at a recent Caregivers Forum held in Colorado Springs, Colorado. He said this statistic was one of many items revealed in a survey of pastors by the Fuller Institute of Church Growth:

80% OF PASTORS INTERVIEWED BELIEVE THAT THEIR PASTORAL MINISTRY IS AFFECTING THEIR FAMILIES IN A NEGATIVE WAY.

Disturbing? Alarming? Yes. But entirely believable. As Evie and I (and our Barnabas International teams) travel the world, Christian leaders often share with us their heartaches pertaining to their families. We've listened, prayed with them, and even wept with them. That's because we've so closely identified with them. We, too, *have experienced personal heartaches* because of restlessness, waywardness, and rebellion with some of our own children. I'm convinced that *nothing hurts the heart of a parent more than this.*

In her book, *Prodigals and Those Who Love Them*, Ruth Bell Graham is tremendously encouraging on this matter. The Grahams are very candid in writing the book as they share their own experience in raising two of their own children who were rebels-- but who have both now returned to knowing, loving, and serving the Lord. The book also gives case histories of many other rebellious youth who ultimately committed their lives to Christ and were significantly used of the Lord.

But back to the statistic--*80% of us in ministry believe that our pastoral ministry is affecting our families in a negative way.*

As I look around, I agree that this is probably accurate. But if so, *why*?

Perhaps our families are being negatively affected because in our zeal to help others, *we are neglecting our own partners and children*. Even as I write this, I feel a sense of real guilt. Perhaps I, too, have given more time, more encouragement, more understanding to others than to my very own.

Or, maybe our families are being negatively affected because Satan's attack is more strategic and effective against the families of Christian leaders. I'm quite convinced that this is a contributing factor. We know that Satan will try to discredit our ministries through our children. Satan will also endeavor to *discourage us*, to cause us to "throw in the towel" through the spiritual disinterest or the unbelief of our own children.

Fellow parents, our ministry is important, but not to the exclusion of our loved ones. Let's covenant afresh to give priority to our families. To love them unconditionally. To pray for them constantly and with great fervor.

And let's be willing to accept *some* of the blame for failures and the negative impact, but let us not accept *all* of the blame.

My dear friend and college classmate, now a well-known psychologist, Dr. David Carlson, has said to all of us who tend to blame ourselves for all of our children's wanderings--*God, too, has some unruly children, but that doesn't mean He's a bad parent.*

> *"Love one another. As I have loved you, so you must love one another. All men will know you are my disciples if you love one another."*
> John 13:34-35 (NIV)

> *"Let us not love with words or tongue but with actions and in truth."*
> 1 John 3:18 (NIV)

FORTUNE COOKIE THEOLOGY

Recently I had a Chinese dinner with a small cluster of ministry friends in Detroit, Michigan. After the dinner we had, of course, the typical dessert--a fortune cookie. As each of us broke open his cookie, we read the notes locked inside. We listened to each other read the tiny slips of paper and chuckled. Occasionally we even laughed out loud. Here's what mine said:

"Good news for you. No more troubles."

Our first response was laughter. Later, I thought about that message. I didn't laugh this time as I thought about it. In fact, my responses changed completely . . . moving through multiple transitions. From the initial chuckle to disbelief--frustration--anger --sadness. And that's where it ended. Sadness because the message of the cookie was absolutely dead wrong. It was a *lie*! That message never was true. Nor is it true now. It never will be true as long as we are earthbound. My feelings of sadness grew as I thought of the hundreds of other people reading that fortune cookie message. If they believed it, they'd be disillusioned. Life on earth *will never be trouble free*. In fact, the opposite is true.

There are two major reasons for denying the philosophy of a trouble-free journey through life:

1. Human Experience Confirms the Reality of Trouble

My own experience affirms the reality and necessity of trouble. My years in the ministry, in the family, and in the workplace have brought a variety of troubles my way. I suspect your experience has taught you similar lessons . . . *trouble* is universal to humans.

133

In the last several months I have met with Christians in Europe, Africa, and South America. If I were to compile a catalog of trouble from around the world that we as Christians must face in our daily experience, it would be lengthy and complex. Marital pressures. Prodigal children. Widespread economic depression. Personal economic pain. Famine and drought. Mental anguish. Nervous breakdowns. Self-doubts and accompanying questions of self-worth. Illness. Incapacitating handicaps. Persecution. Misunderstanding from co-workers. Distractions, deadlines or delays that keep us from being or doing our best for God.

2. Biblical Teaching Confirms the Reality of Trouble

Some of those who are listed in God's Hall of Fame give us first-person accounts of their experiences with difficulty:

JOB: After facing an incredible array of troubles, he cried out, *"the thing which I greatly feared is upon me"* (Job 3:25). Yet, Job states with confidence, *"Though He slay me, yet will I trust Him"* (Job 13:15).

DAVID: When walking through continual opposition and conflict, David often asked the question, *"Why?"* But again and again, he wrote, in the Psalms, *"Bless the Lord, O my soul."* David knew God as One who was faithfully able to deliver him from sin, trouble, and affliction.

PAUL: In writing to his young friend, Timothy, the apostle states, *"All that will live godly lives will suffer persecution"* (2 Timothy 3:12). He reminded his protege, *"The Lord will rescue me . . ."* (2 Timothy 4:18, WILLIAMS).

PETER: As an elderly, triumphant, and realistic believer, he wrote these words of instruction, scattered throughout

134

his first epistle, *"There will be all kinds of trials. . . . Do not be surprised at the painful trial you are suffering as though something strange were happening to you . . ."* (1 Peter 1:7, 4:12).   Yet, the Apostle Peter goes on to say, *"Humble yourselves, therefore, under God's mighty hand that he may lift you up in due time.   Cast all your anxiety upon him because he cares for you"* (1 Peter 5:6-7, NIV).

JESUS: Our dearest Friend reminds us: *" . . . In this world you will have trouble."* Happily, He then adds these words, *"But take heart. I have overcome the world"* (John 16:33).

Troubles will be with us.   Often they may be fierce.   Intense. Persistent. But be encouraged--Jesus will always be with us. Even in the hottest fiery furnace, Shadrach, Meshach, and Abednego had a fourth companion. It was Jesus. He, too, will be with us in every trouble. He has promised it to be true.

> *"Consider it pure joy, my brothers, whenever you face trials of many kinds, because you know that the testing of your faith develops perseverance."*
>
> *"Blessed is the man who perseveres under trial because when he has stood the test, he will receive the crown of life that God has promised to those who love Him."*
>
> *James 1:2-3, 12 (TLB)*

THE VISION THING

Do you believe in dreams and visions? Better yet, are you pursuing or in the process of fulfilling a dream or a vision?

Often in these past several years, Evie and I have found ourselves thanking God for giving us the *vision* for Barnabas International, for planting the dream in our hearts . . . for working in and through us . . . grooming us . . . equipping us . . . and now, for blessing us toward the vision's fulfillment.

Yes, I believe in dreams and visions.

Notice what Peter said on the Day of Pentecost. The apostle indicated that the events of Pentecost ushered in a remarkable era.

"In the last days, God says, 'I will pour out my Spirit on all people . . . on sons and daughters . . . on the young and the old . . . and they will see visions and dream dreams' " (Acts 2:17, NIV).

Dreams . . . visions. It's happened before. It happened in the Book of Acts. It happened throughout early church history. It's even happened in our century . . . and it's happening today. In fact, during these last several months, I have met a number of Christians who are trailblazers for God. They are . . . *"seeing visions and dreaming dreams"* for new ministries.

MARGORY FOYLE . . . from London has served Christ as a psychiatrist. Now, nearing retirement, she travels the world extensively bringing an in-depth ministry to the physical/psychiatric needs of missionaries.

FRANK WINTER . . . from San Diego has resigned a prestigious position as the Director of

136

Ophthalmology at Stanford University. Now he's opening clinics in Africa, ministering to those who are blind, physically and spiritually.

TOM HOY . . . in Warsaw, Indiana, has begun UNLIMITED POTENTIAL, a ministry using major league baseball players to host clinics, and hundreds are receiving Christ.

BILL MOORE . . . from Rockford, a successful practicing Christian attorney, gave up his law practice, enrolled in seminary, graduated, and left the door all the way open, trusting God with not just his own life, but his wife and their four daughters. Bill has said, "Anything, anywhere, Lord."

It's exciting, isn't it? Sometimes the vision starts with a fleeting thought, then a recurring thought, possibly a dominating--even obsessive--thought. The vision is nurtured with prayer and more prayer. Soon you are convinced, "THIS VISION IS FROM GOD AND IT CAN BE ACCOMPLISHED." *Yes, dreams can come true! Visions can become realities.*

Could it be that in the closing years of the twentieth century, we'll see even more individuals with God-inspired visions and Spirit-empowered dreams?

And where are *you* in this process? Are you just beginning to catch a vision of what God has for you? Or . . . maybe you are seeing it quite clearly. You might even be well on the way toward seeing the completion of a vision. Still . . . some of you must rather frankly admit, "I am not sure at all what God has for me."

But surely you want to be involved in God's world view. I want to make a difference. And I think you do, too.

It's okay--in fact, it's wonderful. In fact, I even encourage it. Be a dreamer. Be a visionary for God.

> *"Where there is no vision, the people perish."*
>
> Proverbs 29:18 (KJV)

> *"And it shall come to pass afterward, that I will pour out my spirit upon all flesh; and your sons and your daughters shall prophesy, your old men shall dream dreams, and your young men shall see visions."*
>
> Joel 2:28 (KJV)

MINISTRY HAS RISKS

The other evening, just before being introduced at a Bible conference in mid-Africa, a fellow worker sang something I had never heard before. The message of the song was powerful. It was also incredibly moving and relevant for the large group of Christian workers from at least fourteen different Christian ministries gathered together in Rwanda. Many of these friends are serving in very difficult settings of political instability, civil unrest, economic pressure, evacuations (past and potentially threatening again), and innumerable problems.

Look at some of the words of the song:

> "There marches through the centuries the martyrs of the cross.
> And many chose to follow Christ, to suffer any loss.

138

And though their journey led them through the shadow-
   lands of death,
The song of their commitment they rehearsed with every
   breath.
I will serve the Lord. I will serve the Lord, my God.
And if God should choose, and my life I lose . . .
Though my foe may slay me . . . I will serve the Lord."

As the man sang the song, and as I looked around the room, I knew
the personal stories of many of these heroic servants of the cross.
Many thoughts raced through my mind to confirm the reality and
validity of what was being sung.

~ Several years ago the late missiologist, J. Herbert Kane,
challenged the youth of our generation to set personal goals
aside to accept a "tough assignment" where one might
hesitate taking a marital partner or having children.

~ I recalled hearing the adult choir of a church in China
singing with joy and commitment, *Am I a Soldier of the
Cross?* Somehow they sang it with a conviction and depth
that I lacked. Too often I have flippantly and quickly sung
merely "mouthing the words."

~ I remembered several years ago kneeling at the humble
tombstone of Chet Bitterman, a Bible translator martyred in
Colombia, South America, and rededicating my life to
serving the Lord . . . whatever the cost might be.

~ I thought of the call of Christ to "take your cross daily and
follow Me."

~ I remembered the words of the older apostle Paul writing to
Timothy: " . . . *be strong in the grace that is in Christ Jesus
. . . . Endure hardship with us like a good soldier of Christ*

Jesus. No one serving as a soldier gets involved in civilian affairs. . . . Similarly, if anyone competes as an athlete, he does not receive the victor's crown unless he competes according to the rules. . . . Reflect on what I am saying" (2 Timothy 2:1-7, NIV).

Yes, there is a risk involved in ministry. It hasn't always been easy. Nor will things always go easily. But He has called us to follow *and* to serve Him. Our reward will be given us as we follow Him.

> *"He gives strength to the weary and increases the power of the weak."*
>
> Isaiah 40:29 (NIV)

> *"For this God is our God for ever and ever; He will be our guide even to the end."*
>
> Psalm 48:14 (NIV)

THE QUITTER

I wonder if there isn't a bit of John Mark in all of us--at least the potential for us to *become* another John Mark.

You remember John Mark (nicknamed "the quitter") from the Book of Acts. He was a member of the ministry team with Paul and Barnabas. But the Scriptures tell us that all of a sudden John Mark quit. That's right. *He disappeared.* There are no details given. No explanations. Just a lot of speculation. The Bible simply says that he quit. *Finished.* Over and done.

A Quitter. It was then--and still is--hard to forget or overcome the stigma of such a label. Especially this one--*the Quitter*. The truth is that *most of us occasionally think of quitting.* As I've traveled the world, in personal conversation with friends like you, I often hear confidential confessions of struggles over the temptation to drop out of ministry. Some *have* quit. But others have endured. More have victoriously stuck by their responsibilities.

I remember hearing the testimony of two elderly Bible translators in Central America. They shared their story with a small group of us. Their ministry spanned many decades beginning with a Bibleless tribe. This pair lived with that tribe for most of their adult lives.

Our purpose in meeting with them was to help them celebrate the completion of their task of translating both the Old and New Testaments into the language of the people. But their candid testimony revealed the many times they were tempted to throw in the towel. What a moving story of victory over their inclinations to quit.

If they had stopped, it's possible there was no one else in the world to take their places! Can you imagine?

There are so many factors that might cause us to quit:
    -- the task is beyond our abilities . . .
        -- or maybe it's too tough . . .
            -- or we suffer from "burn-out" syndrome
    -- or a lack of sufficient funds . . .
        -- inability to learn the language . . .
            -- cultural or religious barriers . . .
    -- strained relationships with our coworkers . . .
        -- so few tangible results . . .
            -- chronic fatigue or emotional stress . . .
            -- or even illness.

And don't you see many of these are legitimate issues? There are also weaker, trendy phrases heard too often today--*"I am just not being fulfilled."* Or, *"I don't sense reward."* Admittedly I have a lot of trouble finding legitimacy in that kind of thinking, but it's just as tough to deal with legitimate concerns, like those we all face from time to time.

John Mark--the quitter. But it's unfair to end his story there. Yes, John Mark did quit. Yes, he did spend some time "on the shelf."

But John Mark came back! This story ended with John Mark getting a new label, *The Comeback.* This man had a *new beginning.* This man started over again.

I remember a cartoon that really struck me. The caption said:

> *"If at first you don't succeed, try again. Then quit. There's no use making a fool of yourself."*

A former president of Wheaton College often said, *"It is always too soon to quit."* These words have become a favorite expression of mine (and you'll note that we even chose the phrase for our book title). Frame these words. You may need to remind yourself of them often.

Now a personal word to you:

To you who are now tempted to quit . . .
Share your story with a trusted friend. Be candid in conversation and prayer with this person. Search the Word for God's promises relating to His adequacy for your every need and look for ways around your feelings.

142

To you who have already quit . . .

Is it time to "come back" again? Once you resigned. Perhaps now you should "re-sign" up again. I have talked with many friends who did just that--and they were restored, refreshed, and involved again in productive ministry.

To you who have never quit . . .

Praise God! You already know from experience that it is only by His grace and strength that you have persevered. *Well Done.* Words for you now but someday from *His* lips to you.

> "Never . . . never . . . never . . . never give up."
> --Winston Churchill

BELIEVING GOD MORE

Henrietta Mears, toward the end of her life, said, "If ever I had my life to live over again, I would believe God more."

I was at Arrowhead Springs at the International Headquarters of Campus Crusade for Christ for a *New Life 2000* committee meeting. While there, I stayed in the room dedicated to the life and memory of Henrietta Mears. A colored portrait of her was in the room as was a brief resume of her life on a plaque.

As a young man in my early twenties, I had the privilege of meeting Miss Mears when she was the Director of Christian Education at the Hollywood Presbyterian Church. She brought the

Sunday School attendance from 400 students to over 4,000 students during her leadership in the church. It was at her church that Miss Mears introduced the concept of teacher training. She also founded the Gospel Light Press to provide graded materials to help both teachers and students. She later founded GLINT, recently changed to Gospel Literature International, a foundation to help train Christians in other cultures to evangelize and disciple individuals, providing Gospel literature in native tongues.

When I met Miss Mears, I saw her as a bundle of sanctified energy, deeply committed to Christ--with an eagerness to see people come to Christ and then to grow in Christ. She had a positive impact on the lives of many people, including Bill Bright and Vonette, who later became Bill's wife. Miss Mears led many thousands of individuals to Christ. She pioneered Christian camping and founded Forest Home, a Christian Conference Center in the mountains of southern California. She started the Hollywood Christian Group with its goal of reaching film and TV entertainers with the Gospel of Christ. Henrietta Mears attempted so much for God. And she *accomplished* much for Him.

Yet despite this honor roll of accomplishments, the plaque dedicated to her memory began with her quotation: *"If ever I had my life to live over again, I would believe God more."*

What a challenge to me . . . to Believe God More.

I need to accept this challenge right now. Will you join me in spending some private moments with Him, now, pondering Him-- looking for ways to **believe God more?** There's a need in our lives to believe God for even "impossible" goals and accomplishments.

God is faithful in His nature. *Infinitely reliable.* Trustworthy. All of the Scriptures are *faithful and true.* The promises of the Bible are sound. Steady. Sure. Every prophecy has or shall be fulfilled.

Paul wrote: *"We have the hope of eternal life, which God, who does not lie, promised before the beginning of time"* (Titus 1:2).

Are you ready for a new commitment to Him in this area of *believing Him more?*

Are you trusting Him fully with your ministry?

Trusting Him for the results of your work?

Trusting Him with your children?

Trusting Him with your finances?

Trusting Him with your burdens?

Trusting Him for each aspect of your future?

David said, *"His faithfulness extends into the heavens."* It also extends to you and me--right here and now.

> *"See then that ye walk circumspectly, not as fools, but as wise, redeeming the time, because the days are evil."*
>
> Ephesians 5:15-16 (KJV)

IS IT HARD TO SAY THANKS?

I was in the audience when Mother Teresa spoke at the National Prayer Breakfast in Washington, D.C. Her speech was deeply moving--warm, Biblical, simple, and so convincing because her lifestyle matches her message. She shared the following story with those of us in the audience.

One evening in Calcutta, she and three other nurses went out to minister to people on the streets. They picked up four needy people and took them back to her hospital. Each was in bad shape but one was especially desperate. She said to her colleagues, "You take care of those three. I will care for this one--she looks worse."

Mother Teresa then told us, "I did for her all that my love could do. I put her in bed. There was such a beautiful smile on her face. She took hold of my hand, and she said, 'thank you' . . . and she died."

The Gospels record an event in the life of Jesus where He healed ten lepers. Sadly, only one came back to say "thank you" to Him. I don't know why it's so hard for some people to show gratitude. No doubt your mother, like mine, did her best to train her children. "What do you *say*?", she always prompted us when we were little, as a cue to thank someone. Those were valuable lessons. It's sad when people, organizations, or churches forget to say "thanks."

In contrast, several months ago I observed a recognition service where a man was honored for service to a Christian ministry. He had served over forty years as a board member, sacrificially giving of his time, talents, and money. The time of recognition was appropriate. It was healthy for both the recipient and for the organization to honor him and say "thank you."

Our organization, Barnabas International, is committed to the ministry of encouragement to people in ministry all over the world. Over 6,500 friends receive our letter each month. When we started these letters of *Encouragement* over seven years ago, we hoped that two things would happen. In fact, in my first *Encouragement* letter, I stated that we had two goals in sending out these letters:

1. That we be an encouragement *to you*. We pray often that each issue will be significantly used of God to *encourage you*. All of us need encouragement. I do. You do. So be encouraged right now.

146

2. That you become an encourager *to others*. We are surrounded by people who need encouragement. Your family. Your coworkers. Your friends. Your enemies (defined by Governor Al Quie as *individuals who have offended you*). The Bible constantly reminds us of this primary ministry that is given to all believers--***Encourage one another*** (Hebrews 3:13; 10:25; 1 Thessalonians 5:11).

There's a remarkable book, *Boardroom Confidence*, which I can't get out of my mind. Authors Biehl and Engstrom mention three essential ingredients as necessities in effective Christian ministry and leadership: *appreciation, recognition,* and *encouragement.* I often pray that these three qualities/disciplines will be intertwined in my life and ministry. I long for them to be a part of my lifestyle --as second-nature extensions of my life and ministry.

But these qualities do not come readily. *It is sometimes easier to be a discourager than an encourager.* It is easier to ignore than to recognize. It is easier to take people for granted than to express appreciation.

My friend, Jack Wiens, is an artist. He designed a Christmas gift for me some years ago. It was a motto that said, *If you love someone, tell them so.* Let's do it.

Again--make the commitments to *appreciation, recognition,* and *encouragement.*

> *"Therefore, encourage one another and build each other up, just in fact as you are doing. Now . . . respect those who work hard among you, who are over you in the Lord and who admonish you. Hold them in the highest regard in love because of their work. Live in peace with each other."*
> 1 Thessalonians 5:11-13 (TLB)

WHEN YOU CAN'T "HAVE A GOOD DAY"

When Evie and I returned from an overseas assignment recently, on the flight we read the current issue of an international version of a news magazine. I must admit that most of the news was distressing as the magazine covered events and updates from around the world. It was *not encouraging*, to say the least.

In certain parts of the world there has been some sense of euphoria about THE NEW WORLD ORDER during the past few years. Through some of the efforts of the United Nations, there have indeed been some victories. But I wonder if we haven't placed too much hope in the U.N. efforts.

So, suddenly optimism is usurped by pessimism again. Realism, too. If you study world events and history, you know that the world is *not* in good shape. It is *not* getting better.

After having traveled in over 90 countries, I have some genuine concerns. Not just about other countries. Concern about my own nation also. Our nation has just been rocked by drug wars, riots, drive-by shootings and random violence. Children who want to divorce their parents. Parents who abandon or abuse their kids. Events and human beings are losing their power to shock us with their wildness, violence, or weirdness.

International tension and misunderstanding seem to linger and refuse an easy resolution. Natural disasters have battered our country with unrelenting persistence. An entire scenario is being played out as if scripted from Matthew 24:4-14. Terrorism becomes quiet only to rise again and again.

And it's the same all over the world. The high hopes of change in the former Soviet Union and Eastern Europe have been often frustrated and elusive. Peace in the Middle East continues to be a distant and fragile dream after centuries of tension and struggle. Many of the countries of Africa are living with political, economic, and spiritual disaster. And everywhere we see a proliferation of cults and erroneous "isms."

How do I feel about the future of the world? In the short term I am not optimistic. Of course, *in the long term I am very optimistic.*

These thoughts are based on what I see in the Scriptures. Biblical writers give us a peek or two into the future:

> *People from every tribe and language and nation will be in Heaven* (Revelation 5:9).

> *Jesus will be Lord of all* (Philippians 2:9-11).

> *There will be peace and prosperity* (The Old Testament Prophets).

> *No more tears, death, mourning, crying, or pain* (Revelation 21:4).

Some day--*every day will be a good day.*

But now? You and I are dispersed through the nations of the world in obedience to the call of Christ (Matthew 28:19). We are endeavoring to make a difference by our Christian presence. Others of you are involved in international intercession (Psalm 2:8)

You, too, are making a difference. And still others of you are giving of your finances for the work of Jesus even as friends of our Lord did in the Gospels.

Again, these are globally tough times. Millions of people never have a good day. With Christ, however, our ultimate and temporal life can be enriched and eternal life can be assured.

Let's not lose sight of our task. There is hope. Eternal . . . *hope.*

> *". . . in the last days perilous times shall come."*
> 2 Timothy 3:1 (KJV)

> *"And it shall come to pass afterward, that I will pour out My Spirit upon all flesh."*
> Joel 2:28 (KJV)

> *"And this Gospel of the kingdom shall be preached in all the world as a witness unto all nations; and then shall the end come."*
> Matthew 24:14 (KJV)

GIVE HIM YOUR BEST

A word or two about our vocations. . . .

The other morning I received a letter from a friend who is a doctor in Calcutta, India. Toward the end of his letter he wrote:

> "Please pray for me and my vocational ministry.
> I TREAT, BUT GOD HEALS."

My friend views his vocation in a truly Christian sense. He has the right perspective about his vocation, about his partnership with

God. He worked long and hard to become a skilled doctor, and now works even harder helping to treat people's physical problems.

Yet he recognizes that he is only an instrument . . . only the vehicle through whom God works and heals. For those of us who tend to overly inflate our vocational worth, we need the reminder that we are only clay pots. *But Christ lives in us and works through us*, making use of these "clay pots."

We are partners with God, but He is definitely the **Senior Partner**. Remember His words to His disciples . . . ***Without Me you can do nothing*** (John 15:5).

Several years ago in Guatemala, a maintenance worker assigned to a large mission center shared his testimony with his coworkers:

> "My job here is *not* to fix leaky faucets. Not to repair broken hinges. Not to rewire faulty appliances. But my job here is to ***encourage you*** by fixing leaky faucets--by repairing broken hinges--by rewiring faulty appliances."

This friend also has a healthy perspective about his vocation. He sees his work in relationship to God and to others. He recognizes that through his vocational commitment he is a servant both to God as well as to people.

For those of us who sometimes diminish our own self-worth and underestimate the value of our vocations, God calls us to see our work both in relationship to Him and to those we're called to serve. For as we serve others, we also serve Him. And our commitment to serving Him gives value to our relationships with others.

So for all of us, let us develop Biblically sound *theologies of work*. Let us not think too highly nor too lowly of ourselves--our abilities --our talents--our gifts.

Let's look realistically at what God has given us to do. And let us carry a **Biblical balance** with a full recognition of Jesus' words:

"Without Me you can do nothing" (John 15:5).

But let us remember that it is also true that we are powerful *with* Him and can accomplish much good for Him.

"I can do all things through Him who strengthens me."
Philippians 4:13 (NASB)

The point is . . . whether we are doctors, maintenance workers--or preachers, teachers, or janitors . . . evangelists, church planters, or mechanics . . . linguists, musicians, or typists--*let us serve confidently and gratefully as partners with God.*

Hear ye the Master's call, "Give Me thy best!"
For, be it great or small, that is His test.
Do thou the best you can, not for reward,
Not for the praise of men, but for the Lord.

Wait not for men to laud, heed not their slight;
Winning the smile of God brings its delight!
Aiding the good and true ne'er goes unblest.
All that we think or do, be it the best.

(Refrain)
Every work for Jesus will be blest,
But He asks from everyone his best.
Our talents may be few, those may be small
But unto Him is due our best, our all.
--S. C. Kirk

ACCUSER OR ENCOURAGER?

Some time ago, I finished four speaking assignments at a conference in Indiana where my final message was on *The Ministry of Encouragement*. Following the message, an older gentleman came to me and said,

> "Thank you for your ministry today. Encouragement is an important ministry. I learned that a number of years ago. I used to be pretty hard on people. I was critical. I was adversarial. Definitely a bit nasty and hasty with people. But God changed me and I became **an encourager** *instead of an accuser of the brethren*. What a difference it has made **in me** and **in others**."

What a wonderful testimony. Have you yet made the transition from being an **accuser** to becoming an **encourager**? Have you discovered the importance of this ministry of encouragement? Have you become a partner with God in His personal ministry of encouragement to people?

The ministry of encouragement is important because people need to be encouraged. In fact, you are surrounded by people who need encouragement--family, neighbors, coworkers--everyone. We *all* need it. *You, too, need it.* And the strange thing is, you will find that *encouragement, like the boomerang, will return to you* as you generously give it out to others.

The ministry of encouragement is so important because God has called all of us believers to this ministry. He has given us many explicit commands. For example--

> *"Encourage one another and build up one another."*
> 1 Thessalonians 5:11(NASB)

"Encourage one another daily . . . so that none of you be hardened by sin's deceitfulness."

Hebrews 3:13 (NIV)

"Encourage one another and all the more as you see the Day approaching."

Hebrews 10:25 (NASB)

Sometimes we neglect this ministry of encouragement and these commands with excuses that might sound defensible to us but they are very weak when examined by the Scriptures. We beg off of the ministry of encouragement by saying:

> *It is not my spiritual gift . . .*
> > *It is not something that I'm comfortable with . . .*
> > > *It is not my family trait or ethnic distinction.*
> > > *It is not part of my personality.*

These and other excuses are robbing us and others of the blessings that could come to us and through us if only we would embrace this ministry of encouragement.

Charles Swindoll in his book, *Encourage Me* (Multnomah Press), writes, "I know of no one more needed, more valuable, more Christ-like than the individual who has committed himself to the ministry of encouragement."

He quotes from William Barclay: *"One of the highest of human duties is the duty of encouragement. It is easy to laugh at men's ideals; it is easy to pour cold water on their enthusiasm; it is easy to discourage others. The world is full of discouragers. We have a duty to encourage one another. Many a time a word of praise, or thanks, or appreciation, or cheer has kept a man on his feet. Blessed is the one who speaks such a word."*

Yes . . . it is time to stop being the **accuser**.

And it is time to become the **encourager**.

You can make a positive difference in someone's life today.

> *"Now if your experience of Christ's encouragement
> and love means anything to you, if you have known
> something of the fellowship of His Spirit, and all
> that it means in kindness and deep sympathy, do
> make my best hopes for you come true! Live
> together in love, as though you had only one mind
> and one spirit between you. Never act from motives
> of rivalry or personal vanity, but in humility think
> more of one another than you do of yourselves."*
>
> Philippians 2:1-4 (J.B. Phillips)

"ALL THINGS" . . . REALLY?

Mother Teresa has said, "You will never know that Jesus is all you
need until Jesus is all you have." Again she has stated a most
profound truth, yet has stated it simply.

In the Old Testament, Job discovered God's total sufficiency when
God allowed Satan to strip him of almost everything--his children,
his wealth, his possessions, his health, his wife, and his friends. In
great despair and loss, he had **only** God left. Then, and only then,
Job listened to God. As he listened, he heard God give one of His

155

grandest and most intimate self-revelations. (All of this is recorded in four chapters beginning with Job 38.) Amazing and rich truths about God. And Job's response to God affirmed that when everything else was gone, there was only the Lord who remained-- but HE was enough.

In the New Testament, Paul discovered the same reality and adequacy in the Lord. *When he discovered the Christ, Paul cast off everything else that he had once trusted* (Philippians 3). When the props were gone, *he still stood tall--taller than ever.* He built the rest of his life on the solid foundation of Jesus Christ:

> *"I can do all things through Christ"* (Philippians 4:13).

> *"We are more than conquerors through him [Christ]"* (Romans 8:37).

Paul's life was filled with incredible difficulties but he found Jesus to be *the Friend that sticks closer than a brother.*

How about some current illustrations? Let me look into my mailbag for correspondence received in the last few days:

From an African nation . . . torn with war and terror and killing:

> "Thousands have been killed in our country. Even here on our center, Christian pastors have been killed. We have been burying and burying. Graves are all over our compound."

From Central America:
> "Three of our staff were kidnapped nine months ago. We are praying for their release. Thanks for sending us the monthly letter, *Encouragement.*"

156

From the South Pacific . . . in conversation with a Bible translator
whose husband was murdered six months ago:
"I have discovered that knowing Christ does not give
me a free detour around life's problems but a guided
tour *through* them."

Indeed, Jesus is all that we need. Intellectually, we believe this and
our faith affirms it. Only experience establishes this as living truth.
No longer is it a second-hand phrase. No longer is it distant truth.
No longer is it just mouthing words. Often I have sung the chorus:
"Christ is all I need. Christ is all I need.
All . . . *all* I need . . . Jesus . . . is all I need."
But too often I have just been parroting these words. Still, the
words are true. They are consistent with Biblical teaching. And I
am increasingly finding them to be **living, vital doctrine.**

I think of Jimmy, my 16-year-old friend living in an orphanage in
Bangalore, India. He was abandoned by his family as a "throw-
away." Blind. Deformed body. But--*good news!* After coming to
the orphanage, he came to know Jesus. With a warm smile on his
face he sang, "Oh, how I love Jesus because He first loved me."
Jimmy was still abandoned by his family. Blind, deformed. *But--
he was rich because he had Jesus.*

> Just when I need Him, Jesus is near,
> Just when I falter, just when I fear;
> Ready to help me, ready to cheer.
> Just when I need Him most.
>
> Just when I need Him, He is my All,
> Answering when upon Him I call;
> Tenderly watching lest I should fall,
> Just when I need Him most.
> --Wm. C. Poole

HONK IF YOU LOVE JESUS

Last fall, Evie and I had just returned from a quick two-day trip up into Minnesota and Wisconsin. We love the crisp, cool days of autumn. We were especially fascinated with the movement of multitudes of geese in the air. At times it looked like the birds were swarming haphazardly in the air--just trying to get organized for travel. Evie and I were both in awe with the beauty of seeing the geese "fly in formation" from the north toward the southlands.

I was reminded of something that my friend, Dean Johnson, told me some months ago. He had just finished reading the book, *High Flying Geese,* by Brown Bahn. Dean shared with me these facts:

> *"Canadian geese increase their efficiency by up to 70% by flying in formation."*

The author advanced two major observations/explanations. First, the position of lead goose kept changing. Because of the energy and stresses involved in leading the flock, there's a constant rotation of leadership. The lead goose absorbed much of the brunt of wind fatigue and expended the most energy. Then, the author observed that the birds are constantly honking. The reason for this was not only as a warning, but possibly the excited honking of the geese is meant to be an *encouragement* to each other. They were not alone. They had a sense of belonging. A real community.

There are some powerful lessons here. Yes, leadership is costly. It takes a toll on all of us. The head of any Christian organization knows about pressure, criticism, intense expectations, fatigue, and sometimes even burn-out. There are many valid reasons for *rotating leadership*. All of us leaders need times for renewal and refreshment. Time out for a rest break lest we *do break*. Our organizations also benefit from new voices.

What about the "honking"? Even as the geese constantly "spoke" to each other, we, too, need to be in constant communication with each other . . . and committed to the ministry of encouragement-- *daily*. I have just finished reading Ted Engstrom's excellent book on leadership, *Boardroom Confidence*. He talks to us (at any level of leadership) about three things--**encouragement, appreciation,** and **recognition**. Don't neglect the ministry of "honking" to one another throughout the day.   Honks of **encouragement, appreciation,** and **recognition**. Go ahead; *be a honker!*

Nehemiah illustrates how to get a task accomplished. He provided the vision and leadership to repair and rebuild the walls and gates of the city of Jerusalem. *But he did not do it alone.* He organized helpers to assist with the job. The task began and continued. *It was not easy.* There were delays. *There were detractors.* There was danger. *There was opposition.*   Yet Nehemiah and his co-workers continued toiling side-by-side, each doing his assignment for the overall good of the group and the project. The Scriptures tell us that ***all the people worked with all their heart***.   And amazingly--in 52 days the job was completed.

> The Canadian geese organized for efficiency. Nehemiah organized for efficiency. You and your ministry team must do the same. The call is not to isolation. Nor to solo ministry. The call, rather, is to ***teamwork***.

> *"Serve the Lord with gladness . . . . Know ye that the Lord He is God; it is He that hath made us, and not we ourselves; we are His people . . . . be thankful unto Him, and bless His name. For the Lord is good; His mercy is everlasting."*
> Psalm 100:2-5a (KJV)

BYPASS MEDIOCRITY

Occasionally I read or hear a written prayer that arrests my attention and causes me to want to make that prayer my prayer. Evie and I heard such a prayer recently at the National Prayer Breakfast meetings in Washington, D.C. It was given by Kay Coles James, an aide at the White House. She adapted it from *My Commitment as a Christian*, written by an unknown author.

The prayer is not bland . . . not typical . . . not traditional . . . not stereotyped . . . not "vain repetition." Rather it is fresh . . . genuine . . . powerful . . . meaningful. I find it especially penetrating when I read it *slowly, thoughtfully*, and *audibly,* which is how I first heard it. Perhaps you, like me, will return to it often, making this prayer your prayer as you face the future.

Father, make us a part of the fellowship of the unashamed. Help us to remember we have Holy Spirit Power. The die has been cast. We have stepped over the line. The decision has been made. We're your disciples. We won't look back, let up, slow down, back away, or be still.

Father, thank You that in You our pasts are redeemed, our present makes sense, our future is secure. We're finished and done with low living, sight walking, small planning, smooth knees, colorless dreams, tamed visions, mundane talking, cheap living, and dwarfed goals.

As your leaders, help us not to need pre-eminence, prosperity, position, promotions, plaudits, or popularity. Fill us with Your Spirit so that we don't have to be right, first, tops, recognized, praised, regarded, or rewarded. Help us to live by faith, lean on Your presence, walk by patience, lift by prayer, and labor by Your power.

Father, our face is set, our gait is fast, our goal is heaven, our road is narrow, our way rough, our companions few, our Guide reliable, our mission clear. We cannot be bought, compromised, detoured, lured away, turned back, deluded or delayed. We will not flinch in the face of sacrifice, hesitate in the presence of the adversary, negotiate at the table of the enemy, ponder at the pool of popularity, or meander in the maze of mediocrity.

Help us, Father, to not give up, shut up, let up, until we have stayed up, stored up, prayed up, paid up, preached up for the cause of Christ. We are Your disciples. Help us go 'til You come, give 'til we drop, preach 'til all know, and work 'til **You** stop us. And when You come for Your own, Father, we pray that You will have no problem recognizing us--OUR BANNERS WILL BE CLEAR! Amen.

Many of you are situated in difficult environments. And your work is *hard*. Your ministry is often obscure. Visible results are few. You're surrounded by a society of unbelievers who don't share your ideals. Even within the *Christian* community we notice that some believers are dropping by the wayside from discouragement, moral lapse, distraction, and a host of other allurements.

In times like these, I commit the prayer above and the hymn below to you.

> Then in fellowship sweet
> We will sit at His feet,
> Or will walk by His side in the way;
> What He says, we will do,
> Where He sends we will go,
> Never fear, only trust and obey.
> --John H. Sammis

JESUS IN THE NEWS

It finally happened. Jesus made the cover of U.S. NEWS & WORLD REPORT. It was the cover story of the issue dated December 20, 1993.

However, sadly but predictably, Jesus did NOT get a good review.

The lead article was entitled *Who Was Jesus?* and the subtitle was *A New Look at His Deeds and Words.* Seven pages were given to these discussions.

In spite of some nice things that were occasionally said about Him, the magazine writers generally discredited Jesus and His words were diluted. The authority of the Scriptures was also doubted, diminished, and severely questioned.

For example, let me give you some direct quotations.

As to His Person:
"*Today, as in His own time, Jesus of Nazareth remains one of history's most intriguing and enigmatic figures.*" (Incidentally, the current PEOPLE magazine had a lead article entitled *The 25 Most Intriguing People Of The Year.*) Jesus is more than intriguing. *Infinitely more.*

As to His Miracles:
The magazine said, "*It was a display of magic art . . . calling Him a magician and deceiver of people. Many Biblical experts are convinced that Jesus did not perform all the miracles ascribed to Him in the Gospels. Others also did miracles. Whether or not the specific events recorded in the Gospels are factual accounts of actual events remains a matter of dispute.*"

As to His Stated Authority:
> According to U.S. NEWS & WORLD REPORT, *"It is recorded that He stated, **'I am the promised One.'** The article says that some scholars doubt that Jesus ever spoke these words."*

As to the Biblical Accounts About Him:
> *"All the stories are re-worked,"* says the author of the magazine article.

Initially I was encouraged to see Jesus' likeness on the cover of a major news magazine. However, after reading the article, I was saddened. Not surprised, but saddened.

Things haven't changed much since His physical journey on the earth. Then, too, He was misunderstood. *He came to His own and they did not receive Him. Ignored. Rejected. Opposed.* And--finally nailed to the cross. Finished? Vanished? *Not at all.* Three days later, He reappeared in victory and triumph.

Whether 2,000 years ago or now, Jesus does not *seem* to be having an impact upon the masses. Individuals treat Him variously--from neglect to vigorous opposition. He receives the same treatment from some governments--and even from some of the world's major religious systems.

But there are exceptions. Many exceptions. *Millions around the world are committing their lives to Christ.*

Several months ago, I was in the former Soviet Union in the city of Sumy, the Ukraine. I was staying in a hotel. One morning I left my room singing . . . *"Jesus, Jesus, Jesus . . . there's something about His Name. Kings and Kingdoms will all pass away, but there's something about His Name."*

A stranger, who identified himself as a tourist from Stuttgart, Germany, said to me, "That sounds like a good song but a strange song to be sung in this country."

Not strange. Universally true. Jesus has already been declared the Winner. *We are just waiting for the day of Coronation.* Until then, ***don't be discouraged*** in your ministry. Nor in the response of people to Jesus. Now, as then, the masses will still reject Him. ***But some will believe.*** *Some will love and serve Him.*

> *"He is precious to you who believe."*
> 1 Peter 2:7a (Beck)

> Precious promise God hath given
> To the weary passerby,
> On the way from earth to heaven,
> *"I will guide thee with Mine eye."*
> --Nathaniel Niles

THE MAKING OF MARTYRS

Once I wrote my monthly *Encouragement* letter from mid-Africa, inspired by a new song I heard which included these words: *"I will serve the Lord my God. And if God should choose and my life I lose . . . though my foe may slay me, I will serve the Lord."* When I wrote those words, I didn't know what the next month would bring to me as I traveled to Peru just a few weeks later on another trip for Barnabas International. Let me explain.

On the Sunday before I preached in the Amazonian jungle center at Yarinacocha, Peru, an announcement was made of the death of Romulo Saune. Romulo, age 40, had been an outstanding Christian in Peru. He was a co-translator of the Ayacucho Quechua New Testament. Later, Romulo was involved in the training of leadership, community development, radio programming, and the pioneering of the first indigenous music ministry among the Quechua people.

So, you can see why his death, and more specifically the manner of his death, stunned and saddened all of us. A week earlier, on Saturday, he was on the way to Ayacucho. About twelve miles outside of town, about a hundred armed guerillas set up a roadblock. His vehicle was stopped along with many other autos, trucks, and buses.

No one knows for sure exactly what happened next except that Romulo, his brother, two cousins, and six others were shot. When the gunfire stopped, *ten men lay dead.* The subversives then set fire to many of the vehicles. Soon a police helicopter arrived. In the gun battle that followed, twenty-four subversives were killed while attempting to flee into the hills. Romulo's aged parents watched all of this in horror. Several years ago Romulo's grandfather, a Quechua pastor, was also killed by subversives.

The funeral for Romulo and other family members was held in Ayacucho not far from the killings. It was an incredibly sad but triumphant occasion despite Satan's vicious attack. Over 2,000 attended the memorial service and made up the huge procession that carried the coffins through the city. Over 5,000 people lined the streets as mourners filed by. People reported that Ayacucho had never witnessed such a triumphant funeral procession. Evangelicals carried the coffins of the martyrs on their shoulders and sang songs of praise to the Lord. A Wycliffe member at the funeral stated, "All the subversives standing there must have been trembling in their boots as they witnessed the power of God."

Then, a few days later, an evening memorial service was held in Lima. And I was asked to participate in another memorial service, this time at the Wycliffe center. Romulo's wife is a Wycliffe "MK" who grew up in Yarinacocha. We all experienced a meaningful evening of celebration and tribute to the greatness of our God . . . a steady Rock in time of storm . . . a faithful Friend in good times and in tough times . . . a coming King to reward His saints.

Just three months earlier, Romulo was honored by the **World Evangelical Fellowship** with the 1992 *Religious Liberty Award* at the 9th General Assembly in Manila, the Republic of the Philippines. And as wonderful as this recognition was, there is yet another day of honor coming. Listen to the words of Jesus:

> *"Do not be afraid of what you are about to suffer. Be faithful even to the point of death, and I will give you the crown of life."*   Revelation 2:10 (NIV)

Is there any encouragement in all of this tragedy? A word for you?

Yes. *Be faithful.* Regardless of how things may look at times, Satan is NOT the ultimate victor. JESUS SHALL REIGN. *We, too, shall reign with Him.* So be faithful . . . *through it all.*

> *"I eagerly expect and hope that I will in no way be ashamed, but will have sufficient courage so that now as always Christ will be exalted in my body, whether by life or by death. For to me, to live is Christ and to die is gain."*
>   Philippians 1:20-21 (TLB)

THE FINISH LINE

During the Mexico City Olympics, Mamo Wolde of Ethiopia won the 26-mile marathon.   One hour later, after the crowd had dispersed, John Akhwari of Tanzania crossed the finish line. One of his legs was blood-soaked and bandaged following a serious fall that he had taken earlier in the race that day.   As John hobbled across the finish line, in agony and pain, he limped on to the first aid station. *But he finished the race.*

Later he was asked why he even bothered to finish the race. Didn't he know he couldn't *possibly* win?   John replied, "My country didn't send me here to *start* the race. They sent me here to *finish* the race."

What a great and inspiring illustration of **commitment**!

Perhaps you are serving Christ in a very difficult setting. You're serving Him, but the results are slow . . . *and slim.* Or maybe your health is poor . . . deteriorating. Or your heart is heavy with a burden (perhaps, many burdens) that are heavy. No one seems to understand--or, worse yet, even care.

I just received a letter from a friend whose ministry team has been dissolved. Now he's sorting out emotions, misunderstandings, lack of trust, and uncertainty about the future. He's been stopped cold in the middle of the race and has to consider how--or whether--he should go on. *You, too, might be asking, "Shall I finish the race?"*

Indeed . . . the race isn't easy. There are many things to stop us. Multiple distractions (that go with the turf of life on earth). Unrealistic expectations (from people who want to impose their impossible and often unnecessary codes upon us). It's not easy.

Variable afflictions (making it easy to "honorably" exit the race) threaten us. Persistent sin (which the writer of Hebrews calls "the besetting sin") gets in the way. *Wow*--the whole process sounds tough. Well, hear me clearly--*it often is very tough.*

So what shall I do? As always, the Bible gives us the right guidance. I find Hebrews 12:1-2 and 2 Timothy 4:7-8 especially helpful. From these verses I learn that God calls us--*each* of us:

To Run the Race with Perseverance.
It comes from the Greek, *Hupomone*, which can be translated *patience*, *endurance*, or *perseverance*, a stick-to-it mentality.

To Run the Race with Hindrances Removed.
"Let us lay aside every weight and the sin which so readily entangles us" (Hebrews 12:1). You know your own vulner-abilities. And you know that to succeed, you're going to have to deal with them.

To Run the Race with a Commitment to the Course.
As Paul neared the end of his physical journey, he was able to say, *"I have fought the good fight. I have finished the course. I have kept the faith"* (2 Timothy 4:7). The writer of Hebrews clarifies this by speaking of the *"race marked out for us."* That *personalizes* the issue. Each believer is called into the race . . . and each of us was given an *individualized* course to run.

Like the wounded runner in Mexico City, you may be hurting and bleeding. You're no doubt battle weary and work tired. You are asking yourself some nagging but realistic questions:

> *"Can I keep going?"*
>> *"Can I make it?"*
>>> *"Can I finish the race?"*

I encourage you in times like these to remember Jesus Christ. He ran the race and finished the course. And remember Paul. He ran the race and finished the course. Then remember our runner from Tanzania who said, "My country didn't send me here to *start* the race. They sent me here to *finish* the race."

God did not send me (nor you) here to *start* the race but to **finish** the race. By God's grace we shall stand together one day at His throne and say it together . . . *"We made it. We finished the race."*

Awake, my Soul, stretch every nerve,
And press with vigor on!
A heavenly race demands thy zeal,
And an immortal crown, And an immortal crown.

A cloud of witnesses around
Hold thee in survey;
Forget the steps already trod,
And onward urge thy way, And onward urge thy way.

Blest Savior, introduced by Thee,
Have I my race begun?
And crowned with victory,
At Thy feet I'll lay my honors down,
I'll lay my honors down.

--Philip Doddridge

THE GREATER HEALING

I heard a story that warmed my heart while its message emphasized an important Biblical truth. It seems that during the middle part of the century, a young boy with polio was fitted with a leg brace so that he might walk. The handicap didn't bother him when he was little, but when he had to compete with other boys in school, the boy realized the limitations of that leg brace.

Out of the blue one day he asked his father, "Dad, do you think God can heal my leg?" His dad took him to a church where some other people had been healed and the father and son together sat in prayer. Each in his own way prayed for a miracle.

The boy watched his dad's face as he prayed, and saw that it reflected his faith and hope. Then he looked down and saw nothing had changed with his leg. After their prayers, they left the church, the young boy still struggling as he dragged the afflicted limb behind him. Yet, somehow there *was a difference.* The boy was overcome by intense peace and joy from inside. Although his withered leg was no different, somehow *something* had changed.

He said later, "I can still remember that experience. Right then I knew that I was *healed* . . . oh, not in my leg, but in my mind. So it didn't make any difference that I still had a leg brace and limped, because I now had a mind full of faith and hope!"

That story is a testimony of God's ability to heal. It shows us a *greater miracle* of *healing the inner man* rather than just healing the external man. Indeed, both are demonstrations of God's power and are miraculous. But maybe the former is the *greater* miracle.

The Biblical account of Paul's "thorn in the flesh" shows this truth (2 Corinthians 12:7-10). He knew God could heal him and three different times he prayed specifically for that healing, but God's answer was:

> *"My grace is sufficient for you, for my power is made perfect in weakness."*   2 Corinthians 12:9a (NIV)

And Paul's response to that word from the Lord was . . .

> *"Therefore I will boast all the more gladly about my weaknesses so that Christ's power may rest on me. That is why, for Christ's sake, I delight in weaknesses, in insults, in hardships, in persecutions, in difficulties. For when I am weak, then I am strong."*
>
> 2 Corinthians 9b, 10 (NIV)

Paul was **not healed** of his "thorn in the flesh." *But he was healed in his spirit.* Paul was set free *inside*, **where it counts the most.**

God is in the business of changing people *in circumstances that may not change*. He heals hearts and spirits **but doesn't always heal bodies**. And in your situation, perhaps you face some heavy situations. You've prayed that the *problems would be removed*. Maybe they're physical problems. Financial problems. Relational problems. And despite your praying, the problems are still there.

I am quite convinced that God still hears your prayer, but sometimes chooses to act in a way as to perform a *greater* miracle. If circumstances don't change, pray for God to change *you* instead.

> *"Though I walk in the midst of trouble, you preserve my life; you stretch out your hand against the anger of my foes, With your right hand you save me."*
>
> Psalm 138:7 (NIV)

AVOIDING SUICIDE BRIDGE

When I was in Venezuela in a conference setting with our friends at TEAM, meeting in Rubio, several friends took us to a neighboring town, San Cristobal. We went to see an infamous site called the "suicide bridge." It is a high bridge. A long bridge. Its name has come from the fact that many have jumped from this bridge to a quick death.

Recently some concerned citizens have written and installed a large sign on the bridge to help deter future self-destructors--at least to give them something to think about--and hopefully to turn them back to choosing life over death.

The message on the bridge is written in Spanish. A translation in English, in part, goes like this:

> *"You are worth more than you imagine. There doesn't exist among the millions of beings that live on earth another being like you nor another with the same fingerprints. Don't lose the opportunity to learn and improve yourself more each day, to understand the special and elevated reason that brought you to live on this planet--because you are better than you think you are!"*

You or I might have written a different message, but maybe not-- there is significant truth in the message as it stands.

You might not always be aware of it, but each of us ministers to others in settings where we are surrounded by desperate people . . . persons of all ages, often characterized by feelings of depression, uselessness, meaninglessness, purposelessness, and hopelessness.

Such feelings create a severe plight. An unknown author has said: "One can live without money, fame, and family. But one cannot live without hope."

William Barclay adds, "There are no hopeless situations in life. There are only individuals who have grown hopeless about them."

What is our message to such people? First of all, let's be aware that there are probably *many* such people around us. Maybe even in our own families, in our own circle of associates and service. And just beyond these close circles, there are countless people trapped in hopelessness. They are all around us. Perhaps you and I need an increased *awareness* of this reality. Then there is also the need of *sensitivity* toward them. But moving on--what is our message, as Christians, to these hopeless and despairing friends?

1. There is hope in our God, for He is a *God of hope.* When the Lord Jesus visited earth, He ministered hope to all whom He touched. Many religious systems are devoid of a message of hope but not our Gospel. It is the *"gospel of hope"* (Colossians 1:23).

2. The Scriptures, too, are saturated with *themes of hope.* In fact, Paul says we have *"encouragement through the hope of the Scriptures"* (Romans 15:4). Let's be so "full" of this Book that the overflow of its encouragement will bless those around us as we model its truths to influence and transform them.

3. The Gospel promises *temporal hope*--that is **hope for today.** Hope in facing the trials and perplexities of this day. God cares about every detail of our needs and frustrations. In Him, there is "light at the end of the tunnel!" There is indeed "a silver lining in every cloud." These are not mere cliches.

The good news is that Christian hope is temporal, yes, but *more than temporal* (1 Corinthians 15:19-21).

4. The Gospel promises an *eternal hope*--something that is eschatological, yet to be evidenced in its fullness. Paul speaks of it as *"eternal encouragement and good hope"* (2 Thessalonians 2:16). Yes, the best is yet to be.

5. A vital relationship with the Lord brings *personal hope*. Those who do not have a personal relationship with Christ know it. They are *"without God and without hope"* (Ephesians 2:12). But those who *do* know Christ are different: *"Those that hope in the Lord shall renew their strength"* (Isaiah 40:31).

Our generation needs the constant realization that life is not found in things--money, prestige, possessions, or other temporal elements. Nor can we place our hope in governments and ideologies. All of these are misplaced and will lead to aborted hope. Our hope must be *in Him*. You and I are then called to be **Ambassadors of Hope**. Let us *live in that hope*. Let us *enjoy that hope*. And let us *pass it on*. You and I can make the difference in another's life today.

> *"Praise be to the God and Father of our Lord Jesus Christ! In his great mercy he has given us new birth into a living hope through the resurrection of Jesus Christ from the dead."*
>
> 1 Peter 1:3 (NIV)

> *". . . and be ready always to give an answer to every man that asketh you a reason of the hope that is in you."*
>
> 1 Peter 3:15 (KJV)

CHANGES

Do you recall the amazing events that took place at the beginning of this decade? All of us were shocked with the news coming out of the Soviet Union and other parts of eastern Europe. When Mikhail Gorbachev became the President of the Soviet Union, he initiated a number of measures which forever changed the face of his country and the surrounding countries. Many of us are still amazed by the changes. We never expected to see them happen. Some of us are perhaps still skeptical.

Not long after the initial upheaval in the former USSR, I had the privilege of ministering in both the Ukraine and Russia on two separate occasions. Just before leaving Moscow, a small cluster of friends stood with me within the Kremlin. We had made a visit into one of the six ornate Russian Orthodox churches, all located right in the Kremlin. There were only a few other tourists there at the time so we felt the liberty of quietly singing some songs together. Although our group was small, our music filled the high-domed church with rich, warm sounds. We sang several songs:

> *Alleluia . . .*
> *All Hail the Power of Jesus' Name . . .*
> *Something About that Name . . .*

As we sang Bill Gaither's song, the words carried real significance, given the setting and the crumbling of the system of Communism:

Jesus, Jesus, Jesus . . .There's just something about that Name.
Master, Savior, Jesus . . . Like the fragrance after the rain.
Jesus, Jesus, Jesus . . . Let all heaven and earth proclaim
Kings and kingdoms will all pass away
But there's something about that Name. *

Our eyes were moist with the emotion of the moment. Our hearts were touched with the awesome reality of what we were singing. *Kings and kingdoms will all pass away.* Indeed, we were standing in what had been one of the most intimidating centers of world power, but where the political system was quickly fading--or more accurately completely crumbling. *But there's something about that Name.* The Name of Jesus has withstood the ravages of time and will last forever because He Himself is eternal. When all else has come and gone, there will be that Eternal One who will forever be *King of kings and Lord of lords.*

Paul eloquently discussed the ultimate role of Jesus as universal Ruler:

> *"God exalted him to the highest place and gave him the name that is above every name. That at the name of Jesus every knee should bow, in heaven and on earth and under the earth, and every tongue confess that Jesus Christ is Lord, to the glory of God the Father."*   Philippians 2:9-11 (NIV)

We know from contemporary history that governments change. Leaders come and go. But we can be confident of this one thing: Jesus Christ is the Lord of Heaven. He is at work in history. Soon He shall be *Lord over all.*

Jesus does not want a place in your life.
He doesn't even want prominence in your life.
He wants pre-eminence in your life.
                                        --J. Stuart Holden

FUNDAMENTALS OF THE GAME

It appears to me, as I travel around the world, that there are some believers among us in ministry who are experiencing defeat. No, they're not yet drop-outs--but they're definitely defeated, frustrated, anxious and worn--looking for shortcuts to effective ministry. But before you jump on some new faddish bandwagon going by, let's get back into the *Word* for some guidance.

Former Green Bay Packers' coach, Vince Lombardi, always told his team, "Whenever you get away from the fundamentals, you've gone a long way toward defeat." Every football player must learn the fundamentals of the game. And he must go beyond just *knowing* these fundamentals and be consistent in his commitment in practicing the fundamentals of the game. If this is true in football, I assure you that it is even *more* true in the Christian life.

The leaders of the early church faced a ministry crisis. Coincidentally, it was exactly at the same time that the church was mushrooming in growth. The leaders had too many demands on their time. They were pulled in so many directions that they were losing their effectiveness . . . losing their perspective . . . losing their priorities . . . losing their commitment to the fundamentals.

Consequently, even during the apparent success of a growing church, they were *moving toward defeat* unless they could *recapture the fundamentals*. These early Christian leaders needed to get *back to the basics*. Notice their concern, then see the resolution for their concern:

> *"It would not be right for us to neglect the ministry of the word of God in order to wait on tables . . . . We will . . . give our attention to prayer and the ministry of the Word."*
> Acts 6:2-4 (NIV)

They made a decisive move to get **back to the basics**. And what were the basics? **Prayer** and the **Word**. That's right--**Prayer** and the **Word**.

Back to the Ministry of Prayer:

God's people have always been called to be a people of prayer. *The most effective people in ministry have been people of prayer.* If you are looking for a ministry with eternal results, then get back to the ministry of prayer. Jesus made prayer a priority as did the apostles in the Book of Acts. And the epistles constantly summon us to lives of prayer. Berridge said, "All decay begins in the closet and nothing will make amends for the lack of it." That's right-- *nothing* will ever make up for the neglect of prayer in our lives and in our ministries.

Back to the Ministry of the Word:

All of as believers are to be *people of the Book.* We are to be full of the Word:

> *"Let the Word of Christ dwell in you richly as you teach and admonish one another with all wisdom and as you sing psalms, hymns, and spiritual songs in your heart to the Lord."*
>
> Colossians 3:16 (NIV)

Both professionally and personally, we are to be full of the Word-- deeply committed to it in our daily lives. Yes, practicing a daily quiet time with the Lord is essential in not just *knowing* but *doing* our fundamental exercises in the *Game of Life.*

I can hear your possible response to this. Some of you are saying, "I know that. I've heard that all my life." And others, "That's so basic. Don't you have something new and fresh?"

Well, the problems aren't new or fresh either. These are not issues or questions we've never faced before. And the solutions are known. Yes, they are simple. Yes, they are familiar. But too often neglected.

This is a call . . . BACK TO THE BASICS.

When all else fails, try this--***back to the basics.*** Better, ***before*** all else fails, try this--***back to the basics.***

> *"Therefore, we do not lose heart. Though outwardly we are wasting away, yet inwardly we are being renewed day by day. For our light and momentary troubles are achieving for us an eternal glory that far outweighs them all."*
>
> 2 Corinthians 4:16-17 (TLB)

PERSISTENT PRAISE

It was a perfect day . . . 82 degrees, sunny, blue sky with white scattered clouds. Hundreds of people filled the Florida beaches. There were the typical beach scenes . . . swimmers, sunbathers, yachts, huge ocean vessels in the distance, fearless youth wrestling in the water with power skis, families building castles in the sand, and even the excitement of a shark in the water. This caused a lot of commotion. It could have been an easy distraction.

Evie and I enjoyed the free day on the beach before coming back from ministry to Rockford. Yet even in the commotion, God powerfully spoke to us through the clapping of the waves and through the thunderous crashing of breakers. It was a lesson in praise . . . consistent praise.

Listen to the psalmist as he calls us to the discipline of praise in Psalm 148 (NASB):

> *"Praise the Lord. Praise Him, sun and moon, all you shining stars. Praise the Lord from the earth, you great sea creatures and all ocean depths, lightning and hail, snow and clouds, stormy winds that do His bidding, you mountains and all hills, fruit trees and all cedars, wild animals and all cattle, small creatures and flying birds. . . . let them praise the name of the Lord. Praise the Lord."*

The psalmist reminds us that all nature is involved in giving praise to the Lord: *The shining sun. The singing bird. The rustling leaves.* Even the crashing waves along the beach.

All of this is a reminder for us to also be consistent . . . and persistent in giving praise to the Lord.

It's true--we need to be taught to praise God. It does not come easily to any of us. The natural man resists efforts at praise. It is easier to pout, gripe, grumble, and complain. Not only do we need to be taught to initially praise God, but we also need to be reminded to frequently give Him praise.

As a child, my parents often needed to remind me to say "Thank you." And as God's child, I still need a reminder to say "Thanks."

Sometimes I *do* feel like praising God and at other times I don't. Sometimes it's easy and often it's difficult--especially in the course of our modern activity where life has its twists and turns--hills and valleys--and detours. Praise doesn't always come so readily.

Even now your circumstances may be difficult and filled with despair. At times such as these, it's often tough for you to practice thanksgiving. *But it is always appropriate to give thanks to the Lord.* Praise pleases the Lord. Praise releases God's energies to work in you and to work as well in your circumstances. And. . . *praise changes you.*

Let us also make the ***praise commitments*** that the psalmist made:

> *"I will bless the Lord at all times. His praise shall continually be in my mouth."*
> Psalm 34:1 (KJV)

> *"My tongue shall speak of thy righteousness and of thy praise all the day long."*
> Psalm 35:28 (KJV)

Until I again have the privilege of a stroll on another beach, I'll remember the lessons of the waves, clapping in persistent, energetic offerings of praise. Might *I* be as constant in my praise.

REAL POWER

The entirety of the Scriptures insist that the *secret of the Christian life* is found in our dynamic union with Christ. There is great simplicity in understanding that fact--but equally *great complexity* in our *achieving it.* The Bible says *our life is in the Lord.* Outside of Him there is no life. That's why we are repeatedly told to . . . **"trust** *in the Lord* . . . **rejoice** *in the Lord* . . . **encourage ourselves** *in the Lord."*

As followers of the Lord our own identity is tied to our identification with Him. Our personal security is in Him. Our individual fulfillment is in Him. *Everything* . . . is to be focused on our relationship to Him.

Yet, we quickly and easily seem to forget this basic truth. We wander back into the same old pathways that once led us to dead ends . . . pathways that have by now become ruts. These paths lead us to dead ends, as we walk in those old familiar ways.

I also find that too often we find ourselves drinking again from the same old unsatisfying fountains that the world drinks from. Will we ever learn that these old pathways and fountains *do not satisfy*?

The ancient philosopher was right when he said, "There is a God-shaped vacuum in the heart of every one of us that can only be satisfied with Christ."

I once heard James A. Baker, then Secretary of State of the United States, speak to our National Prayer Breakfast in Washington, D.C. It was a remarkable address. He talked about being in power and in public life in the administrations of former Presidents Reagan and Bush. Then he shared some important personal observations.

He said, "I found early on that having a position of power doesn't bring the fulfillment that many think it does. . . . Having a position of power does not bring inner security or fulfillment. That comes only by developing a personal relationship with God, which for me is personified by Jesus Christ. . . The most important thing I've learned since coming to Washington is the discovery that temporal power is fleeting."

Then Secretary Baker told this personal anecdote about an early morning incident when he was the White House Chief of Staff:

"As my driver turned the car into the Northwest gate, I looked down Pennsylvania Avenue and noticed a man walking alone. He was someone many of you would have recognized--a Chief of Staff in a previous Administration. There he was, alone--no reporters, no security, no adoring public, no trappings of power--just one solitary man, alone with his thoughts. That mental picture continually serves to remind me of the impermanence of power and place."

If we seek our identity in power, position, possessions, pleasures, people, places, appearance, abilities, or anything else, we will forever be found unsatisfied--unfulfilled. And remember, all of these things constantly beckon and often succeed in drawing those of us who are Christians from having a total alliance with the Lord.

The threat will always be with us. But the empty satisfactions from such pursuits will always leave us wanting. Only God satisfies the deepest longings of our hearts.

> *"Let us hold fast the profession of our faith without wavering . . ."*　　　　Hebrews 10:23 (KJV)

GLOBAL CHRISTIANS

John Stott has said, "We must be global Christians with a global vision because our God is a global God."

John the Disciple was the first to use this concept when he wrote, "God so loved the *world*."

As we follow Christ closely and are captured by His love, He gives us a concern and vision for the needs of people around us and even for those distant from us. We become *global Christians*.

A conspicuous characteristic of the global Christian is worldwide intercession. Paul instructed believers to *intercede . . . for all men, especially those in authority.* That is a call to global intercession-- for governmental leaders on the local, national, and international scene. David, more specifically, shares these words from God about world intercession: *"Ask of me and I will give you the nations"* (Psalm 2:8).

Many of us have found Patrick Johnston's book, *Operation World*, to be a very helpful aid in knowledgeable intercession for specific requests for all the nations of the world. And, Wesley Duewel's book, *Touch the World Through Prayer*, has nudged many of us into systematic intercessory prayer for the peoples of the world.

In addition to these worthy aids, let me share something that has been helpful in my intercession.

I am a *collector*. Actually, Evie might not use such a fancy word to describe my fascination with "stuff." I plead guilty to being excessive, perhaps, as a collector. Our home is filled with tokens and mementos from our travels in over 90 countries around the world.

Often when I ponder a purchase in some distant place, Evie will plead, "Lareau, don't get it. We don't have space." Usually, however, she allows me to get "just one more little remembrance."

My office, especially, is filled with all kinds of things, unusual items from around the world:

For example, a tapestry from the Notre Dame in France . . . a painting on papyrus from Egypt . . . miniature panda bears from China . . . an etching from Grunberg in Austria . . . musical instruments from Africa, South America, and Philippines . . . a fan from Malaysia . . . carved ebony elephants from Africa . . . broken pieces of pottery, dug up from the iron age, from Lachish in Israel . . . an alabaster vase from Egypt . . . vases from Greece . . . many simple things from Indian villages and language groups from all over the world . . . a clock from the Ten Boom Clock Shoppe in Haarlem, the Netherlands . . . spears from Indonesia . . . a cowbell from Switzerland . . . and one a most recent prized possession, a chunk from the Berlin wall. And I admit, this is just a *small part* of my "collection."

Why all this stuff? Or some say junk? A personal museum? I must confess the answer to be "Yes" . . . but these mementos also have a very special meaning to me on a regular basis. These collectibles are my global reminders to pray for the nations and the peoples of the world. As I gaze about the room I am caught up immediately in global intercession. Often each piece has additional personal significance which often leads to even more specific prayer for individual people in these nations.

Each of us is finding our own creative ways to keep a global perspective alive in our thoughts and prayers.

"Brethren, pray for us."   1 Thessalonians 5:25 (KJV)

IN THE PITS

All of us occasionally feel *"in the pits."*

After speaking to a group of pastors recently, several of them came to me to talk privately. They shared pressures, misunderstandings, and frustrations in their ministries. These were ministers who were not afraid to stand boldly in their pulpits to proclaim Christ, but they seemed nervous and uncertain as they faced their own future.

Some of them were being criticized, misunderstood, and decidedly not appreciated by their congregations. They were discouraged. Profoundly so. This is not unknown to Christian workers. All of us at times are frustrated or discouraged in our service to God.

U.S. News & World Report (May 28, 1990) carried a cover story about former First Lady Barbara Bush. She candidly talked about her life and her own difficult times. She especially described what she calls a "major depression" which lasted for six months back in 1976. She writes, "I would feel like crying a lot and I really, painfully hurt."

Mrs. Bush also recalled how she eventually came through the depression. She immersed herself in volunteer service to hurting people. She did basic and menial tasks in helping others. She claims that this activity was a part of the therapy that helped her out of her depression. *The secret?* Ministering to others with a focus on others, not self.

Thank you, Barbara Bush, for underscoring a basic Biblical principle that works.

Listen to the words of Jesus as He taught His disciples the principle of ***Giving Oneself Away:***

"For even the Son of Man did not come to be ministered unto but to give Himself a ransom for many."

Indeed there are times when each of us needs to be encouraged, loved, appreciated . . . and to have others tell us so. But, we aren't always able to have others around to encourage us. And besides, we are *not to major on our own needs.* Let me state it in several ways . . .

~ Rather than waiting to be blessed, we are to bless others.

~ Rather than wanting to be loved, we're to show love to others.

~ Rather than longing to be encouraged, we are to take the initiative and become encouragers.

~ Rather than sulking in our own "pity parties," we are to look around us for hurting people and then reach out to lift them.

Yes, even when we ourselves are bruised and battered, there is potential healing for ourselves *and others* as we reach out and touch another in Jesus' name. ***Often in the act of touching another, we, too, are healed and transformed.***

Life is indeed a boomerang. Eventually, what we give to others comes back to us . . . be it positive or negative.

You really can make a difference in another's life . . . and the process can make a profound difference in you, too.

"My little children, let us not love in word, neither in tongue; but in deed and in truth."
1 John 3:18 (KJV)

MAKING A DIFFERENCE

In overseas ministry, I've often felt overwhelmed with the enormity of the physical and spiritual needs of the people. Let me illustrate.

INDIA: My first visit left me exhausted, depressed, and full of grief at the constant sights of such universal poverty.

THE PHILIPPINES: Smokey Mountain, in Manila, left an awesome impression on me. Squatters everywhere. "What can any one person *possibly do*?" I asked.

CHINA: With a population in excess of one billion, I wondered, "How can we ever reach this country with the Gospel?"

LONELY AND DISCOURAGED: These are found all over the world. Probably in your own neighborhood or even your family room. Who will help them?

UNREACHED PEOPLE GROUPS: With some 2,000 language groups still without the Scriptures in their heart language, I ask, "When will we find Christians to learn the language and translate the Bible into that language?"

The world is filled with overwhelming human need. Not just overseas, but right here at home. Where *we* live. Humanly, it often looks impossible. *Where do we begin* to reach billions still without Christ? --in feeding the masses near starvation--in bringing the Bible to people without one? The task even looks impossible.

Years ago I heard this phrase. "I cannot do everything *but I can do something*." Indeed. This world can be a different place if each of us will *do something*.

I heard this story again the other day. A grandfather walked the beach with his grandson . . . a beach literally covered with starfish. Thousands of them. The boy knew the starfish would die out of the water and he started picking them up and throwing them back out into the water. Grandpa said to his grandson, "There are too many of them. It's impossible. You can't make any difference!"

The grandson replied, as he threw another starfish back into the water, "I can make a difference for *this one*."

Truth indeed. When I was a young boy, I remember hearing a song that left a great impression on me . . . *Little is much if God is in it.*

God asked Moses, "What is that in your hand? Will you give it to Me?" Moses had no idea what God could do with his life and his staff. And when Jesus asked the little boy for a couple loaves of bread and a few fish that the boy had, he had no idea what Jesus could do with this small yet generous gift. How surprised he must have been to see the five thousand fed with his little lunch.

When Simon, the unpredictable "wimp" of the Gospels, was renamed "PETER, THE ROCK" by Jesus, he must have wondered if Jesus knew how weak, unsteady, and shallow he really was. But Peter lived up to the Lord's expectations, and this weak reed became a solid rock. Yes . . . *"little is much if God is in it."*

> A PRAYER THOUGHT: *Lord, I am only one person. I cannot do everything, but I can do something. I present myself to You, with all of my limitations, and trust that my gift will be coupled with Your matchless glory and power. Be praised, O Lord. Amen.*
>
> *"But by the grace of God I am what I am . . ."*
> 2 Corinthians 15:10 (KJV)

EPILOGUE

Each chapter of this book was written originally as a monthly *Encouragement* letter from Barnabas International. They were meant to be shared.

You can receive your own copy of *Encouragement* each month by simply writing to Barnabas and requesting it. You will be given a free monthly subscription.

Permission is granted for you to copy the letters and pass them along to others and extending this ministry of encouragement even further.

For information about Barnabas International, and how you might be used of God to bless and encourage others through this work, you may write or call as follows:

Barnabas International
Post Office Box 11211
Rockford, Illinois 61126-1211 U.S.A.

Telephone: (815) 395-1335
Fax phone: (815) 395-1385